Curriculum Planning and Teaching

Using the Library Media Center

by
MARY KAY URBANIK

The Scarecrow Press, Inc.
Metuchen, N.J., & London
1989

British Library Cataloguing-in-Publication data available

Library of Congress Cataloging-in-Publication Data

Urbanik, Mary Kay.
    Curriculum planning and teaching using the library media center / by Mary Kay Urbanik.
        p. cm.
    Includes bibliographical references and index.
    ISBN 0-8108-2148-6
      1. Teachers—Library orientation.   2. Media programs (Education)
3. Teaching—Aids and devices.   4. Libraries and education.
5. Curriculum planning.   6. School libraries.   I. Title.
Z711.2.U7   1989
025.5′678—dc20   89-31683

Printed on acid-free paper

To Peggy, with love

ACKNOWLEDGMENTS

Special thanks to Katherine Mead, district librarian, Martha Wiser, elementary teacher, and Elizabeth Giatas, Gifted and Talented Program Coordinator, for their critical review of the manuscript.

CONTENTS

INTRODUCTION

THIS BOOK WAS written with several, distinct purposes in mind. First, it is intended to help the classroom teacher become a more active and effective user of school library media center services, resources and materials in curriculum planning and teaching. It promotes the integration of the school library media center with the work of the classroom.

The second major purpose is to acquaint the teacher with the general principles and dynamics of the curriculum planning process, and the role the school library media center plays in that process. Various approaches to curriculum design are explored. More specific instructional planning incorporating use of the school library media center is also addressed. In addition to developing a working knowledge of the basic tenets of curriculum planning and development, the teacher will be able to operate from an expanded options base when engaging in the planning process. Greater creativity in planning can be achieved by drawing on the best features of many designs and models, instead of relying only on one that may not be appropriate for all learners or instructional situations.

The concepts presented in this book are useful for both the beginning and the more experienced teacher. Though placed in the context of an elementary classroom setting, these principles can also be considered and applied at the secondary level.

The major goal is to incorporate media center use into the educator's everyday teaching philosophy and methodology, and to forge a lasting pedagogical link between the curriculum planning and teaching process, and use of the school library media center.

MARY KAY URBANIK

vii

Chapter 1

CURRICULUM PLANNING AND THE SCHOOL LIBRARY MEDIA CENTER: INTERACTION

WHY IS IT important to study principles of curriculum planning in conjunction with school library media centers? The reasons are numerous, and have both immediate and far-reaching effects. Immediate effects involve the continued improvement of instruction. Among far-reaching effects is the development of the process of learning how to learn.

Information is the staple of education. Modern age technology has allowed information to be stored, retrieved and presented in many different formats. Organizational systems have been developed to provide ease of access to desired information, in both print and non-print formats. Every school has its own storehouse of information: the school library media center. This valuable tool, literally at the fingertips of teachers, often goes largely unused. If the teacher does not make regular use of the school library media center, then the students, in turn, miss the opportunity to learn important educational skills.

Knowing how to find answers to questions is an essential element of one of the broad goals of education: learning how to learn. Once learned, the skills involved can serve an individual for a lifetime. However, students cannot begin to acquire these skills unless the teacher possesses them and uses them often and purposefully. That is, the skills should always be taught and used within the context of a lesson or unit (this applies to all subject areas), and not as a separate lesson on "library media skills." In this way, the students can see the relationship between their work in the classroom and use of the library media center.

The library media center contains a rich deposit of resources

1

with the capability, when their use is properly planned for, to make learning directly meaningful for the students. Failure to make well planned use of these resources on a regular basis can diminish the richness of the learning experiences for the student.

Definition of Terms

It may be helpful at this point to define several major terms which occur throughout this book:

Curriculum: The definition of curriculum is broad in nature. Essentially, the curriculum comprises all the learning experienced by students within the formal framework of the school. This definition encompasses both the philosophical and applied aspects of curriculum, in the sense that the philosophy of the school forms the basis for the actual planning, implementation, and evaluation of the curriculum. The curriculum is not an arbitrary matter, but represents an orderly set of intentions (a plan) concerning the learning of the students. The exact nature of these intentions may vary somewhat from district to district, school to school, and even classroom to classroom, depending on influencing factors inherent in each situation, and also the varying needs of the students.

In addition to the formal curriculum of the school, there is often a "hidden" curriculum in operation, one that involves the social structures set up by the students themselves. Educators are often not aware of, or do not acknowledge, the presence of this hidden curriculum. But it has not only a major impact on the socialization of the students; it may also involve means devised by students to "get around" the formally planned curriculum. Often, the hidden curriculum has a greater long-term effect on students than the formally planned curriculum of the school.

Curriculum Planning: The terms "curriculum planning" and "curriculum development" are often used interchangeably. Essentially, curriculum planning/development is the *process* of actually devising the plan. The curriculum planning process is a complex one, involving making a series of decisions or choices, and takes into account both internal and external influencing factors (for example, the needs of the students, and the needs of the community).

The curriculum planning/development process is also systematic. The seven-step model developed by Taba (1962) is probably one of the most straightforward of the various curriculum planning models that have been developed:

Step 1: Diagnosis of needs
Step 2: Formulation of objectives
Step 3: Selection of content
Step 4: Organization of content
Step 5: Selection of learning experiences
Step 6: Organization of learning experiences
Step 7: Determination of what to evaluate and of the ways and means of doing it.[1]

Other curriculum planning models are presented in chapter 3.

Instruction: Instruction is the implementation, or delivery, of the curriculum plan. It is the action taken as a result of the curriculum plan, and involves the presentation of planned learning opportunities or experiences. This includes interaction between people, things (media, materials), new places, ideas, or combinations of all of these things. Instruction may not always directly involve the teacher, although the teacher is the one responsible for providing the various instructional opportunities. Students may take part in instructional activities that require them to interact only with certain materials or resources, or the teacher may play a more direct role in instruction by acting as "mediator" or "facilitator" between the student and a specific learning environment.

Although curriculum and instruction are closely linked, there is a necessary distinction between the two. Curriculum development comes first, followed by instructional planning. Curriculum development is broadly based, concerned with major goals and the group of learners as a whole, and is a long-range process. Instructional development deals with specifics, immediate objectives to be met in order to achieve the broader goals of the overall curriculum, addresses the learners on a more individual basis, and is short-range in nature.

---

[1]Hilda Taba, *Curriculum Development: Theory and Practice* (Harcourt, Brace and World, 1962), p. 12.

School Library Media Center: This is best defined as "An area or system of areas in the school where a full range of information sources, associated equipment, and services from media staff are accessible to students, school personnel, and the school community."[2] Perhaps even more importantly, the library media center is viewed as "A learning laboratory providing all types and kinds of instructional media essential for the optimum support of the educational program. . . ."[3]

The work of the library media specialist is closely linked to that of the teacher, particularly in a curriculum planning and instructional context. Library media specialists, like classroom teachers, receive preparation in curriculum and resource unit planning, and are obliged to be familiar with the curriculum at each grade level of the school they serve. The working relationship between the teacher and library media specialist should be the strong link in the connection between the curriculum planning process and the use of library media as a part of this process. Therefore, the importance of teachers and library media specialists working closely together in curriculum planning cannot be over-emphasized. Communication between teacher and library media specialist regarding specific materials is fine, but it is not enough. The broader basis of communication between teacher and media specialist should be that of the curriculum plan. This requires an understanding of the dynamics of the curriculum planning process itself. Working with the school library media specialist in this context on a continuing basis will help the teacher in better determining appropriate methods, activities, and materials for more innovative learning experiences for the students. This team approach is an aid in the continual improvement of the quality of instruction.

Broad Goals

In exploring the relationship of the school library media center to curriculum planning and teaching, four broad goals emerge.

---

[2]American Library Association and Association for Educational Communication and Technology, *Media Programs: District and School* (Chicago: ALA and AECT, 1975), p. 111.

[3]Ruth Ann Davies, *The School Library Media Center: A Force for Educational Excellence,* 2nd ed. (New York: R. R. Bowker Co., 1974), p. 465.

These goals provide a sense of direction, and unity among the different areas addressed throughout this book. They should become a part of every educator's basic teaching strategies:

A **knowledge** of both printed and audiovisual materials appropriate for the age groups with whom the teachers work. This includes operational skills, and participation in activities (workshops, in-service, etc.) that will serve to keep teachers informed of materials and resources available, and effective ways of using them.

A **familiarity** with and understanding of the criteria and sources used in the selection and evaluation of materials and resources. This will help ensure that materials and resources are used for educational purposes, and not entertainment. Related to the selection criteria is an understanding of the organizational schemes of school library media centers, and proficiency in skills of location and retrieval, allowing teachers easy access to resources.

An **understanding** of the contributions that the school library media center and its staff can make to the total educational program of the school. This necessitates a view of the school library media center as an integral part of the curriculum, not an ancillary, and proper use of the school library media center as a tool in teachers' own curriculum planning. Also included here is an understanding of the need to continuously study the curriculum of the school, the library media facilities, resources, and services, and the needs of the students in order to ensure that the school library media center is being used in the best possible way within the total school program.

An **awareness** of the teacher's function in relation to the library media center's program. This includes working with the library media specialist to develop a library media skills curriculum that is closely related to classroom work. In addition, the teacher should also look continuously for opportunities to make use of various materials, resources, services, and techniques for the purpose of continually improving the teaching-learning situation.

Objectives

These four broad goals are broken down into a number of more specific objectives. The objectives fall into three categories: **knowledge** (facts, content, concepts, generalizations), **values** (affects, viewpoints, attitudes) and **techniques** (processes, skills, abilities). These categories are interrelated, and there are an equal number of objectives in each category. This provides for balance between the categories, and emphasizes the fact that each category shares equal importance with the other two. Figure 1 shows the relationship and balance among the three categories.

The objectives from each category are presented below so that the reader can begin to formulate a conceptual base for curriculum planning and teaching in which the school library media center plays a major role. The objectives do not stand alone; they interlock to form the larger teaching-learning pedagogical structure.

The objectives in the knowledge (facts, concepts, content, generalizations) category are these:

A) A basic knowledge of the history, development, and philosophy of the school library media center.

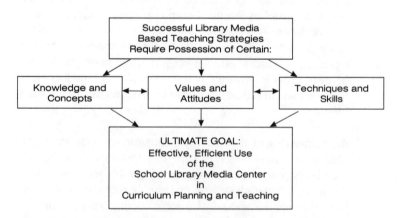

FIG. 1: Relationship and Balance Between the Categories of Objectives Leading to Comprehensive Attainment of the Broad Goals

B) An understanding of what comprises the curriculum planning process and how the process works.
C) Knowledge of the fundamentals of instructional design.
D) Knowledge and understanding of ways to solve instructional problems through use of the library media center.
E) Familiarity with the types of media, materials, resources, and services available through the library media center.
F) Familiarity with selection and evaluation guidelines for media and materials.
G) Familiarity with Loertscher's taxonomy of school library media center involvement in instructional units.

The objectives in the values (affects, viewpoints, attitudes) category are as follows:

A) Knowledge of ways in which to make the school library media center central to classroom learning, and realize its integral place in the total school curriculum.
B) Understanding the importance of the development and use of a library media skills curriculum taught in direct relation to classroom work.
C) Understanding the importance of communication and teamwork with the librarian on an on-going basis, not only to keep informed of new materials, etc., but to improve curriculum planning and teaching.
D) Understanding the place and role of the school library media center within the curriculum planning process.
E) Understanding the importance of the use of media and materials for the right reasons: to educate, not entertain.
F) Recognition and understanding of the value of the use of appropriate media and materials best suited to a particular instructional situation or group of learners.
G) Recognition of the need to continually study the school program (curriculum) to determine whether or not the library media center is being used as effectively as possible.

These are the objectives in the techniques (processes, skills, abilities) category:

A) Information access skills for purposes of research, refer-

ence, professional growth, teaching these skills to students, and continually improving the quality of classroom teaching.

B) Understanding the basic organizational schemes of library media centers, so as to be able to operate in them
more efficiently.

C) Demonstration of competence in the use of a wide variety of media, materials, and resources.

D) Demonstration of the ability to create and/or modify media and materials for specific learning situations.

E) Understanding and ability to demonstrate effective ways
of making use of media, materials, resources, and services in the teaching-learning setting.

F) Demonstration of competence in the total curriculum
planning process.

G) Demonstration of competence in applying the fundamentals of instructional design.

Advantages of Media Center Use

The school library media center exists to help provide for curricular needs, individual student needs, and teachers' professional
needs. However, Erikson states that "Only when teachers know
and understand the many ways in which media can contribute to
their day-to-day efforts, can they be truly interested in and commit-
ted to their effective utilization."[4] Erikson also discusses several
different roles that audiovisual media play.[5] An examination of
some of these roles will help provide a sharper focus on the overall
use of school library media center materials, resources, and services within the curriculum planning and teaching context:

- The teacher has available many ways in which to extend
the "horizon of experience" of the students. Learning by
doing is much more effective than learning by listening
only. A working model of a seismograph set up on a classroom table top allows for direct experience, as opposed to
listening to a lecture on how and why one works.

[4]Carlton W. H. Erikson, *Administering Instructional Media Programs* (New York:
Macmillan Co., 1968), p. 108.
[5]*Ibid.*, pp. 108–111.

- The teacher is able to provide the students with a variety of "meaningful sources of information." Both audio and visual materials are available in varied formats. In addition, there are learning experiences such as field trips and simulations where direct involvement is a key ingredient in the learning process. Opportunities for meaningful learning are greatly increased through consistent, well planned use of library media center materials, resources, and services. Meaningful learning stays with the student.

- Well planned use of library media center materials, resources and services can also help the teacher in providing guidance and direction to individualized or small-group learning situations. Independent research work on a particular topic can make use of a variety of print and non-print sources, individual task cards, and individualized CAI (computer assisted instruction), to cite one illustration of the use of library media materials, resources and services to provide purpose and sequence to the learning experience.

- Careful, well planned use of media and materials can provide interesting and varied ways to introduce a new unit, concept, or lesson. For example, presentation of a film about the sun and planets could be used to open a science unit on the solar system.

- One of the most intriguing aspects of making use of different types of media, materials and resources is that it can be "the means of overcoming physical difficulties of presenting subject matter." Use of such things as movies, pictures, maps, and three-dimensional models can provide adequate substitutes for direct experience when the nature of the topic makes it impractical or impossible for students to experience it directly.

- Another aspect of media and materials use involves the ability to produce one's own when needed or wanted. Groups or individuals (teachers as well as students) working on their own means of conveying information do so with a very distinct sense of purpose. Not only do they learn media and materials preparation and production skills, they also learn how to organize information, and gain a deeper sense of understanding and appreciation of their subject matter. Activities of this nature can be carried out in the lower as well as the upper grades, although older students are likely to produce somewhat more sophisticated materials than their younger counterparts.

The different roles of school library media materials, resources and services discussed above are all intended to be viewed within the larger framework of the curriculum plan. The curriculum plan is the instrument used to determine instruction, and it is the implementation of this plan that sets instruction in motion.

Curriculum planning can be thought of as the *macrocosm* within which the *microcosm* of instructional planning resides. A similar relationship exists between instructional planning and learning materials and resources. The instructional plan should be the determinant in the selection and use of learning materials. "The way in which facts, generalizations, and skills are organized for teaching, and the emphasis upon particular values, have a definite bearing on the way media are selected and put to work."[6] If the materials determine the course the instruction takes, then there has probably been no pre-planning involved. Goodlad makes the following comment on this problem:

> I wish we had some kind of Hippocratic oath to remind us always to keep solid principles of learning, teaching, and education at the center and to guide us in choosing what follows from them.[7]

The solid principles of learning, teaching, and education that Goodlad refers to are embodied in the curriculum planning process, which is the first step in the development of the formal educational program. The choice of appropriate instructional experiences stems from this.

The teacher knows the students best, the library media specialist knows the materials best, and their curricular basis of communication should allow for the best match to be made among students, learning experiences, and the materials and resources needed to

---

[6]Erikson, *Administering Instructional Media Programs*, p. 101.

[7]John I. Goodlad, "Educational Leadership: Toward the Third Era," *Educational Leadership* 35 (January 1978), p. 332.

make the experiences vital. Teachers and library media specialists who work together throughout the entire curriculum planning process will know exactly what is needed to make the best match.

Translating the curriculum into the instructional setting requires the selection and use of appropriate media, materials, resources and library media center services to serve as the vehicle for the learning experiences. "A teacher's goal should not be to lengthen the chain of teaching materials, but to strengthen the chain of experiences through which learners develop intellectually and emotionally and reach learning goals."[8]

The curriculum only comes alive through instruction, and the vitality of the curriculum itself is directly linked to the quality of the learning experiences. Incorporating the use of the school library media center as an essential component of the curriculum planning process ensures that the quality of learning will be at its best.

Summary

Interlocking the school library media center with the curriculum planning process will help in the continuous improvement of the quality of instruction. However, in order for this improvement to be realized in its fullest sense, both the classroom teacher and school librarian need to be operating on the same basic principles.

Definitions of the terms curriculum, curriculum planning, instruction, and school library media center have been provided. The curriculum plan forms the broad basis for interaction and communication between teacher and librarian. The goals and objectives that govern the relationship between the school library media center and curriculum planning have also been presented. Objectives fall into three categories: knowledge, values and skills. Balance between these categories is essential.

Some of the advantages of use of the media center in instruction have been discussed; they include being able to provide a variety of learning modes for the students.

The curriculum plan is the initial framework established. It will determine the direction and nature of the instructional plan. The choice of appropriate media and materials is based on the purpose

---

[8]Walter A. Wittich and Charles F. Schuller, *Instructional Technology: Its Nature and Use*, 6th ed. (New York: Harper and Row, 1979), p. 244.

and objectives of the instructional plan. Opportunities for active use of the school library media center within this framework are many.

References

Erikson, Carlton W. H. *Administering Instructional Media Programs.* New York: The Macmillan Co., 1968.

Lundin, Roy. "The Teacher-Librarian and Informational Skills: An Across the Curriculum Approach," *Emergency Librarian,* 11 (September–October 1983): 8–12.

Posner, George J., and Rudnitsky, Alan N. *Course Design: A Guide to Curriculum Development for Teachers.* 2nd ed. New York and London: Longman, 1982.

Prostano, Emanuel T., and Prostano, Joyce S. *The School Library Media Center.* 3rd ed. Littleton, Colo.: Libraries Unlimited, Inc., 1982.

Saylor, J. Galen, Alexander, William M., and Lewis, Arthur J. *Curriculum Planning for Better Teaching and Learning.* 4th ed. New York: Holt, Rinehart, and Winston, Inc., 1981.

Shapiro, Lillian L. "Media Power and Teacher Liberation," *Catholic Library World* 48 (July–August 1976): 14–20.

Shepherd, Gene D., and Ragan, William B. *Modern Elementary Curriculum.* 6th ed. New York: Holt, Rinehart, and Winston, Inc., 1977.

Shores, Louis. "Library-Trained Teachers," *The Phi Delta Kappan* 22 (February 1940): 303–306.

Taba, Hilda. *Curriculum Development: Theory and Practice.* New York: Harcourt, Brace, and World, Inc., 1962.

Unruh, Glenys G. *Responsive Curriculum Development: Theory and Action.* Berkeley, Calif.: McCutchan Publishing Corporation, 1975.

Chapter 2

DEVELOPMENTAL BACKGROUND AND PHILOSOPHY: SCHOOL LIBRARY MEDIA CENTERS AND CURRICULUM PLANNING

Development of the School Library Media Center

THE CONCEPT OF the library is an old one. Since the beginning of civilization, information has been recorded in one form or another for purposes of preserving knowledge, transactions, and events. It was only logical to devise organized ways of storing this information in a central location, so that it could be retrieved as needed or desired. Libraries, meaning organized stores of records and information, have been in existence since ancient times. However, the invention of the printing press in the fifteenth century had a profound and lasting effect on the development of libraries as they are known today. This shift away from the slow, laborious hand-copying process of the Middle Ages allowed more books to become more accessible to ever-increasing numbers of people.

School libraries in the United States can trace their development back to the early nineteenth century. As early as 1835, for example, New York State voters put into effect a law allowing school districts to levy taxes specifically for school library use. These early libraries consisted of small collections of reference books. The founding of the American Library Association (ALA) in 1876 demonstrated the continued and growing interest in libraries.

During the early part of the twentieth century, emphasis in education was on the mastery of subject matter, largely through the use of a single textbook, recitation and lectures. Though libraries were not considered highly essential in this type of teaching meth-

13

odology, room libraries were already in existence. The 1899 *Addresses and Proceedings* of the NEA recommended the following:

> A collection of fifty books in a room chosen with reference to the age and ability of the pupils in that room is the most satisfactory means of forming a taste for good literature.[1]

The year 1925 saw the *Fourth Yearbook of the NEA, Department of Elementary School Principals,* "Elementary School Library Standards," later published by the American Library Association. This included a comprehensive detailing of elementary school library standards, and represented the beginning of the shift toward the centralized elementary school library media center of today. It was pointed out how easily a classroom could become cluttered up with various materials (magazines, victrola records, etc.) that could distract from the work to be done. The importance of having a "centralized agency" where these materials could be stored and be readily available when they were needed was indicated.

A major developmental factor also occurring at about this time was change within the structure of the school curriculum itself, as a shift from emphasis solely on subject matter to an increased emphasis on the learner began to take place. John Dewey was an early pioneer of this movement, and its effects on the curriculum of the public schools are felt to this day. Concern with the individual student's needs, interests and abilities began to move toward the forefront. The present concept of the school library media center provides educators with ways of meeting these needs, interests and abilities that were never before possible.

As elementary school libraries developed, they remained essentially book libraries. However, concurrent technological developments were taking place which were eventually to have a profound effect on the concept of the library, and on education itself. In the first half of the century, non-print media and their potential use in education were yet to be explored, and held little interest for educators. Books were the basis of education, and would remain so for some time to come.

The period spanning 1941–1958 saw vast growth in the use of

---

[1]Margaret L. Brewer and Sharon O. Willis, *The Elementary School Library* (Shoe String Press, 1970), p. 3.

media and audiovisual methods in educational settings. The military made extensive use of them for training purposes, and following World War II there was a burgeoning period of media use in education. This was a carryover from military (and wartime industrial) training methods. After the war, many teachers coming out of the service and back to the classroom began requesting various media and materials (tapes, records, films, slides, transparencies, etc.) that they had used in the military. It was at this point that non-print media and the accompanying technology began to truly make their way into educational practices, though school libraries still maintained their traditional role as storehouses for books. Further impetus toward elementary school library development was provided by the founding of such professional organizations as the American Association of School Libraries (1951). However, the convergence of print and non-print materials into one central location known as the "school library media center" did not come about until later.

The 1957 launching of Sputnik acted as a catalyst for dramatic change in the perception of education, and of what its priorities should be. This was the era that saw the passage of federal legislation which spurred the growth of the school library as never before. The National Defense Education Act of 1958 appropriated funds specifically for the building of resource materials collections in various curriculum areas. But it was the passage of the Elementary and Secondary Education Act (ESEA) of 1965 that provided the greatest spark for the growth and development of the elementary school library, more so than any other previous stimulus.

Title II of this act provided funds for the purchase of a variety of materials. However, it was up to the local education agency to provide facilities, staffing, and the equipment necessary for the use of audiovisual materials. Title II did not solve school library problems, but it did point up needs and inequities among school library programs on the national level, and was instrumental in helping begin to firmly establish the concept of the school library as integral to the total school program, rather than a peripheral option to be employed only occasionally.

Federal legislation (particularly ESEA) providing funding for school libraries has been by far the most influential factor behind the changes that have taken place in school libraries over the years. However, there have been other important factors. Publication in

1960 of the American Library Association's *Standards for School Library Programs*, followed in 1969 by the ALA and NEA joint publication, *Standards for School Media Programs*, provided a strong shaping force for the modern school library. Brewer offers several other reasons for changes in the school library that have transformed it to the centralized media center of today:[2]

- Emphasis on the learner, instead of the teacher. A fixed body of knowledge can no longer be taught since the advent of the knowledge explosion. Students need to learn how to find information and continue to learn for themselves.

- Individual differences between students. "The facilities and resources available in the school library assist in individualized instruction."

- Technological change. There is now available a wide variety of non-print media where there were once only books.

- Changes in curriculum content and design. There has been a shift away from rigid subject matter areas, and a move toward more child-centered learning.

- Changes in methods of instruction as a result of curriculum changes. This has resulted in a shift away from large-group instruction as the sole means of teaching, and a move toward small-group or individual instruction.

- Education as a leisure activity, formally recognized as early as 1918 in the Seven Cardinal Principles, has moved into even greater prominence due to societal changes. Students need to know how to use their leisure time wisely and well. The library provides myriad opportunities for doing so.

- Need for information. Students need to learn skills enabling them to find the information they need.

---

[2]Joan Brewer, "The Educational Role of the School Library," in *School Librarianship*. Edited by John Cook. (The Pergamon Press, 1981), pp. 37–50.

The late 1960s and early 1970s were a period of partial slow-down after the initial spurt of school library media center growth fostered by federal legislation. Now that library media centers are an established fact of educational life, the next step is for educators to learn how to integrate these centers' materials into their curriculum planning and teaching.

Libraries are an essential part of our educational system as it presently exists. The forms, purposes, functions, programs and services of the earliest school libraries have changed as the school library media center came into being and changes in the curriculum occurred. Taylor has identified two formative phases of development of school library media centers that have occurred thus far, and identifies a third phase that they are moving into. The first phase was the unifying of the book and media collections into a central location. The second involved a concern with specifications regarding facilities, equipment, collections and staff. "A third logical and potential stage for continuing development would seem to lie in stronger alliance with the purposes and strategies of instruction in the individual classroom."[3] Although Taylor made this third projection more than ten years ago, it still is far from being common educational practice.

Philosophical Basis of the School Library Media Center

The primary purpose of organized education is to teach the individual to think and to translate that thinking into a pattern of logical, productive, purposeful behavior. Thinking does not occur in a vacuum; it requires raw materials from which to fashion thought. The various abilities that comprise the thinking process cannot be developed in isolation. They must be developed in conjunction with one another through the use of appropriate materials in well planned learning situations.

John Dewey identified five steps (criteria) that comprise reflective thinking and that serve as the basis for the construction of individual learning experiences. The first criterion is that of interest, in a situation or activity. This is followed by a problem perceived within the situation, which the individual feels compelled to solve.

---

[3]Kenneth I. Taylor, "Media in the Context of Instruction," *School Media Quarterly* 4 (Spring 1976), p. 224.

Next, information pertinent to the problem is gathered and analyzed. This is followed by the formulation of possible solutions to the problem, which are then tested by application to the situation or activity to assess their validity. An essential ingredient of this process is the ability to find, analyze, and synthesize ideas. In the context of a structured educational situation (school), this means that materials must be available, and the individual must possess the skills to explore them thoroughly.

School library media center resources are the materials with which to stimulate creative, significant thinking; they constitute the stuff from which thoughts and ideas are shaped and fashioned. The school library media center and its staff supply not only the raw materials but can also provide the tools, incentive, guidance and climate essential to encourage the creative thinking that should be an element of any learning situation. It is every student's right to have the opportunity to learn the skills necessary in order to make use of the many types of resources and materials needed for creative, independent thinking.

Not only is it every learner's right, but as a contributing member of society, it is his responsibility. Whether used for the formal pursuit of educational goals, or for purposes of independent judgment and decision-making, the ability to locate and use needed information involves a set of basic skills which all responsible members of society should possess.

Libraries are major storehouses of information in our society. However, in order to be able to use them effectively, one needs to understand how information is organized, and how to retrieve it.

Instruction in the effective use of libraries and their resources should begin in the early years of a student's schooling and continue throughout the entire formal educational process. Only then can individuals be thoroughly prepared in the independent information retrieval skills that are essential to sustain life-long personal and professional growth as a contributing member of society.

Continual personal and professional growth is characteristic of those who recognize the importance of life-long learning. Such individuals realize that learning is a key factor in the continual improvement of "quality of life." With the ever-increasing body of knowledge available to the general population, the effectiveness of learning has become more important than ever before. Possession of skills in information retrieval and use is directly related to effective learning. Results of effective learning are evident not only in the individual's self-improvement, but also in the quality of the contributions made to the society at large.

Basic knowledge in the retrieval and use of information and resources consists of more than simply being familiar with a listing of the resources available. Because of the tremendous growth in the quality and quantity of resources and materials for teaching and learning available today, it is increasingly recognized that materials and resources must be introduced to potential users. Consideration must also be given to the *ways* in which educators and learners can make use of these materials and resources.

Essentially, it is a matter of bringing people and information together. Educators who pride themselves on using only a few materials and resources because those are the ones they have always used are doing a great disservice to their students. Learner access to a variety of resources and materials is largely governed by the extent of teacher knowledge of these resources and materials. The number of opportunities for learners to interact with ideas, information, materials and experiences is often determined more by the teacher's knowledge in this realm than the learner's own interests, abilities and needs.

Learning how to learn is becoming increasingly recognized as one of the most important skills for a student to master in the educational process. Less emphasis is being placed on the knowledge of facts, and more on how to locate and use information when needed or wanted. This was recognized over 25 years ago: " . . . an educated man is not only one who knows many facts but one who knows where he can find them."[4]

As teachers encourage development of these skills in their students, they are equipping them with tools that are becoming increasingly essential as our society moves into a post-industrial "information age." The importance of this, particularly in light of future projections for our society, is illustrated in the following statement: " . . . the growing realization that knowledge is search-[ing] and not merely a body of facts and information."[5]

---

[4]Eleanor E. Ahlers, Robert L. Amsden, and Frank N. Philpot, "How to Use the Library to Improve Instruction," *National Association of Secondary Principals Bulletin* 45 (April 1961), p. 228.

[5]Daniel Tanner and Laurel N. Tanner, *Curriculum Development: Theory into Practice*, 2nd ed. (New York: Macmillan Co., 1980), p. 525.

Curriculum History

As with school library media centers, the concept of curriculum planning has developed over a period of time. Curriculum planning as a field of study began to emerge about 1920. Prior to that, Dewey, in *Democracy and Education* (1916), described a systematic rationale for the construction of learning experiences that was to become the basis for much of the thought concerning curriculum planning. The rationale is best presented in Dewey's own words:

> . . . the important thing is that thinking is the method of an educative experience. The essentials of method are therefore identical with the essentials of reflection. They are first that the pupil have a genuine situation of experience—that there be a continuous activity in which he is interested for its own sake; secondly, that a genuine problem develop within this situation as a stimulus to thought; third, that he possess the information and make the observations needed to deal with it; fourth, that suggested solutions occur to him with which he shall be responsible for developing in an orderly way; fifth, that he have opportunity and occasion to test his ideas by application, to make their meaning clear and to discover for himself their validity.[6]

Following in Dewey's footsteps was Franklin Bobbitt, who wrote *The Curriculum* (1918), often referred to as the first actual textbook in the field of curriculum. This coincided with the publication of the report of the Commission on the Reorganization of Secondary Education, *Cardinal Principles of Secondary Education*. Commonly referred to as the "Seven Cardinal Principles," they are just as relevant today as they were when first published in 1918. The Cardinal Principles were an important milestone in the history of curriculum planning because they placed emphasis on the needs of students in relation to their contribution to, and successful functioning in society, rather than on the acquisition of a body of knowledge through the mastery of facts. The principles are as follows:

1) health
2) command of fundamental processes
3) worthy home membership

---

[6]John Dewey, *Democracy and Education* (New York: Free Press, A Division of Macmillan Publishing Co., 1916), p. 163.

4) vocation
5) citizenship
6) worthy use of leisure
7) ethical character.

Bobbitt wrote another book in 1924, *How to Make a Curriculum*, in which the influence of the Seven Cardinal Principles is evident. In this book, Bobbitt defined ten major fields of human experience to be considered in curriculum construction. They are remarkably similar to the Seven Cardinal Principles:

1) language activities
2) health
3) citizenship
4) general social contacts
5) keeping mentally fit
6) leisure occupations
7) religious activities
8) parental responsibilities
9) unspecialized practical activities
10) vocational activities.

The primary concern of Dewey and Bobbitt and those who followed their principles was to provide children with an education that would be practical in nature and could be applied to everyday life. Dewey, in addition to his work with the idea of the curriculum as the construction of learning experiences, or a reconstruction of life experiences, also was the first to point out (in *The Child and the Curriculum*, 1902) the three fundamental sources of all educational objectives: the learner, the society, and the body of knowledge. It is these three factors that form the basis upon which all curriculum decisions are made. However, problems arise when one of these factors becomes dominant over the other two. An equal balance and interaction of these three sources of educational objectives is essential to the construction of a curriculum best suited to the learner. The concept of balance in the curriculum will be further discussed in chapter 3.

The development of the curriculum planning models which are commonly accepted and used today began in the 1940s. The well known Eight-Year Study was pivotal in the development of sound models for curriculum planning. The curriculum report of the Eight-Year Study (*Exploring the Curriculum,* Giles, McCutchen, and Zechiel, 1942) presented four fundamental questions to be applied to any program of curriculum development. These questions represented different yet interrelated areas of concern in curriculum development: 1) What is to be done? (what objectives are to be met?); 2) What subject matter will be used? (what topics, concepts and ideas will be presented?); 3) How will it be organized, and what methodology will be used? and 4) How will the results of this particular plan be evaluated?

In 1949, Tyler, in *Basic Principles of Curriculum and Instruction,* set forth his model for curriculum planning. It became known as the "Tyler Rationale," and is still regarded as a focal point in the field today. It had a major impact on the later development of various models, and its influence is seen even in more recently developed models. In fact, the development of many later curriculum planning models appears to consist of, for the most part, elaboration on this basic planning scheme to a greater and greater degree rather than actual changes within the scheme itself. Because it has had such a profound effect in the field, it is presented here in its original form:

1. What educational purposes should the school seek to attain?

2. What educational experiences can be provided that are likely to attain these purposes?

3. How can these educational experiences be effectively organized?

4. How can we determine whether these purposes are being attained?[7]

Although the "Tyler Rationale" has been subjected to various criticisms from time to time (for example, that it is too "mechanized" and overlooks the learner, or that it is outdated for present use), Tyler has made a most important and long-lasting contribution to the field of curriculum. He was the first to point out the need for a systematic approach to curriculum planning, and the importance of that contribution cannot be disputed.

---

[7]Ralph Tyler, *Basic Principles of Curriculum and Instruction* (University of Chicago Press, 1949), p. 1.

The rationale is a useful tool in helping teachers orient and focus their thinking regarding curriculum planning. It is simple and straightforward, and serves well as an organizing device for interrelated curriculum and media center planning. It can also be helpful in preventing the arbitrary use of school library media center resources and materials in teaching.

Relationship of the Library to Curriculum Planning

What is the relationship of the use of the library media center to the curriculum, and to the curriculum planning process? Krug stated that, " . . . curriculum consists of the means of instruction used by the school to provide for student learning experiences leading to desired learning outcomes."[8] He indicated that these means of instruction include, among other things, the school library. A brief examination of the curriculum planning process in relation to use of the school library media center follows.

At what stage of the curriculum planning process does the school library media center come into active play? All sound curriculum planning is based on the determination of valid goals and objectives for the learners. Actual curriculum content is derived from the stated objectives, and from here appropriate learning experiences are determined. It is at this point that the teacher's skills of library media selection and use are applied so as to provide the richest, most appropriate learning experiences possible. Saylor, Alexander, and Lewis outline the following steps in the curriculum planning process:[9]

1. goals, objectives, and domains

2. curriculum designing

3. curriculum implementation (instruction): "Decisions as to instructional modes made by the responsible teacher(s). The curriculum plan includes alternative modes with suggestions as to resources, media, organization, *thus encouraging flexibility*

---

[8]Edward Krug, *Curriculum Planning*, rev. ed. (New York: Harper and Brothers Publishing, 1957), p. 3.

[9]J. Galen Saylor, William M. Alexander, and Arthur J. Lewis, *Planning Curriculum for Schools*, 3rd ed. (Holt, Rinehart, and Winston, 1974), p. 27.

and more freedom for the teacher(s) and students." [writer's emphasis]

4. curriculum evaluation

Clearly, the school library media center plays an important role in the implementation and "delivery" of the curriculum. Use of the center provides for innovation and creativity in carrying out the curriculum plan.

Summary

Historical and philosophical background information has been presented on both school library media centers and the foundations of curriculum planning. It is important to have an awareness of influencing factors that have led to present-day viewpoints and perspectives in each area.

Developments in the two areas have run parallel for a long time, and have only recently begun to intersect. This intersection represents new directions in educational planning, and the nature of the learning experience.

The development of the school library media center resulted, in large part, from reactions to outside events and circumstances. For example, the launching of *Sputnik* triggered a series of events that had a direct influence on the development of present-day centers in which all types of materials are housed in one location. Library media professionals have long recognized the myriad learning opportunities afforded by such an arrangement. Teachers and curriculum planning specialists must also come to recognize and act upon these possibilities.

An introduction to the curriculum planning process has also been presented. Curriculum planning and development is a long-term process concerned with the larger structure of the total school program. Instruction taking place within the larger curriculum plan addresses the more immediate, day-to-day learning activities taking place. The "Tyler Rationale" forms the basis of many of today's curriculum planning models. Although it is simple in its outward appearance, further study reveals a significant historical background in its development. Factors to consider in curriculum development—the learner, the society, the content, and the importance of maintaining a balance among them—are acknowledged. The curriculum planning model is intended to serve as an organizational device. As educators embark upon their work, the planning model will help keep them from becoming lost in a sea of details. It helps maintain a focus on the goals that have been established, and provides the planning with the direction it needs in order to be successful.

Curriculum planning and development is a discrete field of study. The intent here is only to provide a broad overview of the field, and to present some of the basic concepts regarding curriculum with which all educators should be familiar. This will help improve the quality of planning and provide the basis for strengthening the ties between the curriculum and the school library media center.

References

Bennie, Frances. *Learning Centers: Development and Operation.* Englewood Cliffs, N.J.: Educational Technology Publications, 1977.

Brewer, Joan. "The Educational Role of the School Library," in *School Librarianship.* Edited by John Cook. Pergamon Press, 1981, pp. 37–50.

Brewer, Margaret L., and Willis, Sharon O. *The Elementary School Library.* Shoe String Press, 1970.

Chisholm, Margaret E., and Ely, Donald P. *Media Personnel In Education: A Competency Approach.* Englewood Cliffs, N.J.: Prentice-Hall, Inc., 1976.

Dewey, John. *Democracy and Education.* New York: The Free Press, A Division of Macmillan Publishing Co., Inc., 1916.

Encyclopedia of Educational Research, 5th ed. S.V. "Media Use in Education," by Warren F. Seibert and Eldon J. Ullmer.

Krug, Edward S. *Curriculum Planning.* Revised ed. New York: Harper and Brothers, Publishers, 1957.

McBride, Dr. Otis. "Libraries Have Developed into Media Centers Since World War II," *School and University Review* 1. Colorado University, Boulder, School of Education, 1971.

Raths, Louis. *Teaching for Learning.* Charles E. Merrill Publishing Co., 1969.

Saylor, J. Galen, Alexander, William M., and Lewis, Arthur J., *Curriculum Planning for Better Teaching and Learning.* 4th ed. Holt, Rinehart, and Winston, Inc., 1981.

Sutherland, Louise. "School Library Legislation at the Federal Level," *Library Trends* 19 (October 1970): 192–199.

Taylor, Kenneth I. "Media in the Context of Instruction," *School Media Quarterly* 4 (Spring 1976): 224–228+.

Tyler, Ralph W. *Basic Principles of Curriculum and Instruction.* Chicago: The University of Chicago Press, 1949.

Chapter 3

THE CURRICULUM PLANNING PROCESS

The Curriculum Planning Process: Some Representative Models

THE VARIOUS CURRICULUM planning models discussed in this chapter are presented in chronological order of development, so that thought regarding curriculum planning can be traced from its earlier stages to the present day. In this way, similarities between the models can also be seen. It is notable that the premise upon which each model is based is essentially the same, and has merely been elaborated upon to varying degrees.

The first model is the "Tyler Rationale." As stated in chapter 2, Tyler's model was the first to present a concise, straightforward manner in which to approach curriculum planning. It is simple, but important:

1. What educational purposes should the school seek to attain?

2. What educational experiences can be provided that are likely to attain these purposes?

3. How can these educational experiences be effectively organized?

4. How can we determine whether these purposes are being attained?[1]

This model represents the synthesis of the work done in the field

---

[1]Ralph Tyler, *Basic Principles of Curriculum and Instruction* (Chicago: University of Chicago Press, 1949), p. 1.

of curriculum (as a formal area of study) during the first half of the twentieth century. Many others had made major contributions to the field, but it was Tyler who pulled all of the various contributions together into one concise, representative statement. His work, in turn, influenced the work of others. Taba's seven-step approach to curriculum planning was a direct outgrowth of the "Tyler Rationale." Although it rests on the same foundation, it is somewhat more precise and clearly states an aspect not so readily discernible in Tyler's model. Taba has made a point of specifically including an indication that the needs of the learners must be assessed prior to the development of objectives. Although Tyler addressed this in *Basic Principles of Curriculum and Instruction,* it is not made explicit in the rationale itself. The Taba model is shown below:

    Step 1: Diagnosis of needs
    Step 2: Formulation of objectives
    Step 3: Selection of content
    Step 4: Organization of content
    Step 5: Selection of learning experiences
    Step 6: Organization of learning experiences
    Step 7: Determination of what to evaluate and of the ways and
            means of doing it.[2]

Tyler suggested, as have many past and present authorities in the field, that the objectives for the curriculum arise from three primary sources; studies of the learners themselves, the society in which the learners live, and studies of the various subject matter disciplines. He also suggested the use of philosophical and psychological "screens" in the selection of objectives. As with needs assessment, they are not readily apparent in the rationale itself, though they are discussed in *Basic Principles of Curriculum and Instruction.*

Taba, while stating the need for diagnosis explicitly, does so primarily from the perspective of the learner. It is her contention that the learners need to be studied carefully in order to " . . . diagnose the gaps, deficiencies, and variations"[3] in their backgrounds. This, in turn, will provide the data necessary to make informed,

---

[2]Hilda Taba, *Curriculum Development: Theory and Practice* (Harcourt, Brace and World, 1962), p. 12.
    [3]*Ibid.*

reasonable decisions concerning the selection of appropriate objectives upon which to build the curriculum.

Saylor, Alexander and Lewis devised a planning model with a continuous feedback loop indicated for the design, implementation, and evaluation portions of the model. The model is yet a further refinement of the original "Tyler Rationale," and shows an increased degree of sophistication in keeping with present-day principles and techniques.

(1) BASES (External Variables)

(2) GOALS, OBJECTIVES, AND DOMAINS

(3) CURRICULUM DESIGNING—Decisions as to design(s) made by the responsible curriculum planning group(s) for a particular school center. Various prior decisions by political and social agencies may limit the final design(s).

(4) CURRICULUM IMPLEMENTATION (Instruction)—Decisions as to instructional modes made by the teacher(s). The curriculum plan includes alternative modes with suggestions as to resources, media, organization, thus encouraging flexibility and more freedom for the teacher(s) and students.

(5) CURRICULUM EVALUATION—Decisions as to evaluative procedures for determining learner progress made by the responsible teacher(s). Decisions as to evaluative procedures for evaluating the curriculum plan made by the responsible planning group. Evaluative data become bases for decision making in further planning.[4]

The bases of the curriculum are those mentioned earlier: the learners, the society, and the realm of knowledge. Additional external forces cited by Saylor, Alexander and Lewis include such things as legal requirements to be met, research, and professional knowledge.[5] The goals and objectives of the plan are derived from the combination of factors suggested above. Domains are identified as a "grouping of learning opportunities planned to achieve a single major set of closely related educational goals with corollary sub-

---

[4]J. Galen Saylor, William M. Alexander, and Arthur J. Lewis, *Planning Curriculum for Schools*, 3rd ed. (New York: Holt, Rinehart, and Winston, 1974), p. 27.

[5]J. Galen Saylor, William M. Alexander, and Arthur J. Lewis, *Curriculum Planning for Better Teaching and Learning*, 4th ed. (New York: Holt, Rinehart, and Winston, Inc., 1981), p. 29.

goals and specific objectives."[6] Examples of domains include: personal development, social competence, and continued learning skills.[7]

Another model is one developed by Doll. In *Curriculum Improvement: Decision Making and Process,* Doll states that his is, once again, a revision of Tyler's original model. However, like the Saylor, Alexander and Lewis model, it represents a degree of sophistication and concern with additional factors impinging upon the curriculum planning process not found in the earlier models of Tyler and Taba. Doll's model is presented below:

(1) State the need for your proposed design. Base your statement on a preliminary investigation of need. Think of need as being educational, social, and/or developmental.

(2) Indicate the objectives the design is to serve. State a few prime or major objectives of the design, making them succinct and clear. Be sure that each objective has at least two major parts: an indication of what is to be done and an indication of how you will know when it had been done.

(3) Say what subject matter content will be used within the design; then say how the content will be organized for teaching and learning.

(4) Provide examples of learning experiences that pupils will have—sometimes thought of as pupil activities—using the subject matter content indicated above. Show just how these experiences will be organized to profit pupil learning.

(5) Say *what* you will evaluate, according to your objectives and *how* you will evaluate it.

(6) Show how you will attempt to convince other persons, including persons both in your school and outside it, that they should try the design themselves. Consider publishing the design for the benefit of others.[8]

An interesting concept in Doll's model, not found in the other three models, is the suggestion that the plan be published for the benefit of others. A plan developed to meet the needs of a particular situation is not intended to be applied in its original form in a

---

[6]*Ibid.,* p. 32.

[7]*Ibid.,* p. 33.

[8]Ronald Doll, *Curriculum Improvement: Decision Making and Process,* 5th ed. (Boston: Allyn and Bacon, Inc., 1982), pp. 167–168.

different situation. However, there may be certain principles, techniques, and structures that work well in more than one situation, and that can be adapted and applied successfully in more than one setting. Sharing a plan may help another group of planners arrive at solutions to problems inherent in their own educational settings that they may never have found otherwise. Sharing a plan can be done on a local level through the school library media center. Or, a more broadly based system such as ERIC (Educational Resources Information Centers) will make such information available to anyone who wants it.

In an era when the storage and retrieval of information has become highly efficient, educators have access to a continually growing knowledge base as never before. It is to their advantage to make use of it, and it is one good foundation upon which teachers and library media specialists can build a beneficial working relationship.

Use of the school library media center is an essential part of the total curriculum planning process. The library media specialist and the classroom teacher should work together at every phase of the process in order to develop a solid, well-rounded plan. The library media center itself plays an increasingly active role as the curriculum moves from development to implementation. It should be an integral part of instructional processes and procedures. The depth and richness of the learning experience can be increased in direct relationship to the extent of library media center use.

The principles involved in the curriculum planning process are generic in that they are utilized by all educators in a wide variety of settings and circumstances. The teacher and the librarian, as educators, use these principles to form the basis for their cooperative communication and planning interactions.

A Closer Look at Basic Curriculum Planning Principles

Goals and objectives are always of primary concern in the development of a curriculum plan, and are addressed in the early stages of the planning process. However, two of the models discussed earlier specifically state that *need* must be established first. Valid, reasonable goals and objectives result from careful study of an educational situation in order to identify areas that need improvement. A needs assessment will help in formulating the sharp, clear objectives that shape the rest of the plan.

Once the need for the plan has been determined, goals and objectives are set. Goals involve broader, more long-range final outcomes to be attained, while objectives deal with more immediate, shorter-range outcomes, leading back to the broad goal(s) of the plan.

Ideally, preliminary planning, in which needs are determined and goals and objectives defined, should be done as a cooperative effort by both the classroom teacher and the school library media specialist.

Once the goals and objectives have been set, the next step is to determine the design for meeting them. Organizational strategies are developed as the scope and sequence of the curriculum plan is determined. The scope of the curriculum plan indicates what content will be presented. The sequence indicates the order in which the content, through a variety of learning experiences, will be presented. Ways of meeting the objectives of the curriculum plan need to be determined, and different strategies for doing so developed. This is the point in the curriculum planning process at which the school library media center becomes more visible, through the determination of the materials available to be used in attaining the objectives. The selection and organization of learning experiences and their attendant materials and resources are linked directly to curriculum implementation (instruction).

A final consideration in the planning process is that of evaluation. Simply stated, the basic goal of evaluation is to ascertain the value or worth of something. Although evaluation is visually indicated in each of the four models presented earlier as occurring at the end of the planning process, evaluation strategies are employed throughout the process. The ideal evaluation model assumes two modes, formative and summative. Formative evaluation is ongoing evaluation, that is, it is considered at each and every step throughout the entire planning and implementation process. Summative evaluation occurs at the culmination of the plan, and examines each part of the whole and how well the parts "fit" together. It also addresses itself to the final outcomes of the "activated" curriculum plan. Comprehensive evaluation strategies make use of both formative and summative modes concurrently. They act as a check to keep planning efforts on target, and help prevent them from straying in their focus.

Too many plans are developed only to be filed away on a shelf or in a drawer upon completion of the written portion of the planning. The more clearly defined the purpose of the plan, the greater the chances of successful implementation. An additional point to consider is that the users of the plan should be the same people who originally determined the need for the plan. An individual acting in a coordinating or leadership role who does not necessarily have direct contact with the learners can provide a sense of objectivity contributing to the development of a balanced plan. The use of outside leadership also depends, in part, on how experienced the teachers and library media specialist are in curriculum planning. If the need for the plan is determined solely by an outside agency, the chances for smooth implementation of the plan and a high level of success may be diminished.

Involving from the beginning those who will be using the plan will increase their sense of "ownership" of the plan. Those who devised the plan will see it as a viable means of solving an existing instructional problem. They may not view a plan mandated by an outside agency in the same light. Those who devise a plan on the local level will also be more familiar with the subtleties and nuances of the situation. These can include such things as: the nature of the learners, the capabilities and limitations of the actual physical facilities, the availability of appropriate materials, and the extent of the need to create or develop one's own materials.

Each component of the curriculum planning model must "fit" with the components that precede and follow it. Although the four models presented earlier may at first appear to be linear, with set beginning and end points, in reality they represent a continuum. Curriculum planning is a continuous, ongoing process. Once the process has been set in motion (with the starting point usually being the determination of a need or problem to be addressed), it does not "end." As the plan is developed and put into use, it is continually refined and modified as needed, in addition to being continually evaluated, as long as a particular educational program is in effect.

Evaluation of the curriculum plan and evaluation of instructional outcomes are two different things. Evaluation of instructional outcomes determines the extent to which the actual results correspond to the intended outcomes (objectives). Evaluation of the curriculum plan examines the validity of the plan, the soundness of its structure, and the appropriateness and necessity of each of the components. Saylor, Alexander, and Lewis raise several questions to consider when evaluating the curriculum plan.[9] They relate to all components of the curriculum planning model, and should be given careful consideration by the teachers and media center personnel working on curriculum development. Evaluation criteria include an examination of whether or not use of the curriculum plan is fulfilling the purposes for which it was designed. Also, the validity of the purposes should be appraised. The appropriateness of the plan for the students must be assessed. In terms of content and instruction, is the content the best that could be selected in light of the objectives? Are the instructional strategies directly related to the goals and objectives of the plan? "Are the materials recommended for instructional purposes appropriate and the best available for the purposes envisioned?"[10]

The needs of each new group of learners may vary somewhat, and the goals and objectives of the plan need to be adjusted accordingly. Because each component of the plan is linked to the one both before and after it, a modification of the objectives is likely to require a corresponding modification of the instructional strategies and the accompanying materials. Ways of evaluating pupil progress may also be revised. Evaluation strategies related to learning outcomes may include the following: testing, formal and informal observation of learners, learner self-evaluation, peer evaluation, and evaluation of student projects or products resulting from the learning that has taken place.

Evaluation, however, must also be undertaken in the broader terms of the curriculum plan itself. As components and materials of and for the plan are developed and tested, their results are assessed. Suggestions for improvement and the strengthening of weak areas are made and implemented. A continuous cycle of appraisal and replanning makes it possible for the curriculum plan and the attendant instructional program to be continuously improved. This ongoing procedure provides a sound basis for judgments and decisions regarding the curriculum, which in turn contribute to the development of a quality instructional program.

The importance of evaluation throughout the curriculum devel-

---

[9]Saylor, Alexander and Lewis, *Curriculum Planning for Better Teaching and Learning,* p. 317.
[10]*Ibid.*

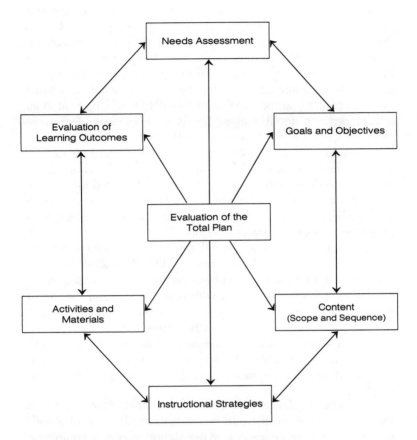

FIG. 2: The Curriculum Planning Continuum

opment and implementation process cannot be over-estimated. The time and effort put into evaluation is well justified in that it systematically leads toward the improvement of teaching and learning, and provides a firm foundation upon which to make informed decisions about the curriculum.

Figure 2 illustrates how all components of the basic curriculum planning model are part of a continuum, and not a strictly linear sequence.

Balance in the Curriculum

The sources of the curriculum can be found within the needs and interests of the learner, the values and problems of society, and the realm of organized knowledge, or subject matter. Literature on curriculum suggests that a balance among these three sources is an important factor to consider when developing any curriculum plan, and is in the best interests of the learners. A strong emphasis on one of the three areas at the expense of the other two will result in an imbalanced and unstable plan. This is a common problem, most often evidenced in the focus on subject matter to be "covered." This approach is often undertaken without true regard for its relevance to the child, or its relationship to the social conditions under which the child may live. Caswell points out the need for " . . . a procedure that generates helpful material from all three sources so that teachers can draw on each to make the wisest selection of experiences in working with students."[11]

An emphasis on the learner will result in much attention to the individual, and materials for students will differ depending on needs, interests and ability levels. Emphasis on the society focuses on the ways in which people interact with one another, and the use of multiple resources is likely to be a part of the course of learning. A stress on subject matter operates on the assumption that there exists a common foundation which everyone must acquire. Materials and resources would most likely be the same for all students, and learning would tend to be more other-(teacher) directed than self-directed.

Achieving a balance among the three sources of the curriculum requires flexibility on the part of the teacher. The use of a wide variety of teaching techniques, materials and resources contributes to this flexibility. Cooperative planning and working with the school library media specialist is another way to achieve this necessary balance.

Differences Among Curriculum Planning, Curriculum, and Instruction

The curriculum planning process is dynamic. It involves the activation of all the elements in the models discussed earlier in this

---

[11]Hollis L. Caswell, "Persistent Curriculum Problems," *The Educational Forum* 63 (November 1978), p. 107.

chapter: assessing needs, determining objectives, selecting content and learning experiences, and evaluating outcomes.

The curriculum may be thought of as a structured series of intended learning outcomes. Part of it is the written, tangible product of the curriculum planning process. The other part is the intangible plan itself in motion. Structure is an essential characteristic of any curriculum. Structure refers not only to temporal sequence within the curriculum, but to the hierarchical relationships between various (content) elements of the curriculum as well.

Instruction is the implementation, or delivery, of the curriculum. The curriculum serves as a guide for instructional direction; it provides the statement of learning intentions. Instruction can be thought of as acting on those intentions. The learning outcomes resulting from instruction in a balanced curriculum plan generally fall into the same three categories as the objectives discussed in chapter 1. These are **knowledge,** or facts, concepts, and generalizations; **techniques,** or processes, skills, and abilities; and **values,** or affects, viewpoints, and attitudes. The categories are not rigidly defined, but are all interrelated; each one affects the other two. As with the three sources of the curriculum, a balance among these three types of learning outcomes is desirable.

Figure 3 clarifies the relationships among the three distinct elements of curriculum planning, the curriculum, and instruction, all of which lead to the learning outcomes.

Beauchamp summarizes the distinction between curriculum and instruction in a most succinct manner. His statement relates directly to use of the school library media center as a central element in curriculum planning and instruction. "Whereas the primary curriculum question is 'What shall be taught in the schools?' the primary instructional question is 'How shall it be taught?' Parenthetically, one should include the choice of instructional materials of all kinds with the 'how to' question."[12]

Organizing Principles

As teachers and library media specialists move to activate the components of the curriculum planning model, certain organizing

---

[12]George A. Beauchamp, "A Hard Look at Curriculum," *Educational Leadership* 35 (February 1978), p. 405.

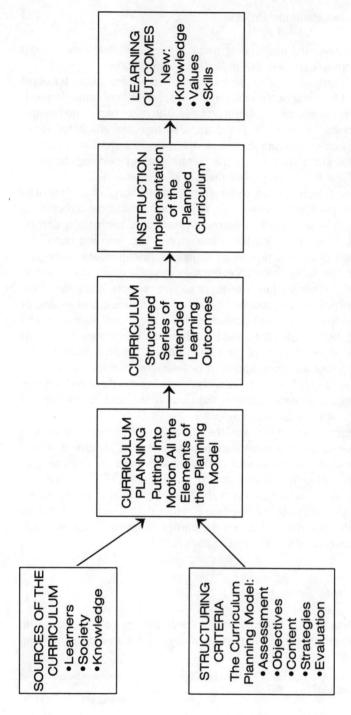

FIG. 3: The Relationship Among Curriculum Planning, Curriculum, and Instruction

principles should be considered within the scope of the entire curriculum development process. Curriculum development is dynamic and ongoing, always subject to modification for continual improvement, and these principles should serve as helpful guidelines in this continuous process of development, modification and improvement. Shepherd and Ragan list six different principles to serve this purpose.[13] They are discussed here in light of cooperative curriculum planning by teachers and library media specialists.

1. When planning curriculum, it is often easy to "forget" the students. This principle is a reminder to keep the students up front in the planning process. In maintaining this perspective, the organization of the curriculum must always take into account the principles of quality, equality, relevancy, and personalization. Shepherd and Ragan define each of these four terms this way:

> Quality is the development of a curriculum which promotes pupil growth in the areas of intellectual, psychological, physical, and social development. Equality is the inclusion of quality experiences for the full range of pupil variations in these same areas. Personalization is the assignment and allocation of the programs to the specific set of individual differences to be instructed. Relevancy is the presenting of a special environment appropriate to the pupil, the society, and the purposes of the school.[14]

2. The organization of the curriculum should be such that it helps to coordinate the efforts of teachers and library media specialists. Their work needs to be interrelated. What takes place in the library media center should be a logical extension, or complimentary part, of what takes place in the classroom. The reverse is also true. This can only result from cooperative planning efforts on the part of both the teacher and the library media specialist.

3. A well balanced school day should be provided the students through curriculum organization efforts. A wide variety of learning experiences that complement each other, and a variety of teaching strategies, should be employed. A balance between quiet activities and those that are more intense should be planned for.

---

[13]Gene D. Shepherd and William B. Ragan, *Modern Elementary Curriculum*, 6th ed. (Holt, Rinehart and Winston, 1982), pp. 76–78.
    [14]*Ibid.*, p. 78.

4. The organization of the curriculum should take into account the continued development of the child, and provide experiences designed to promote that development. Again, the teacher and library media specialist working together will be able to develop a much wider range of learning experiences and activities designed to help the child meet the goals and objectives of the curriculum than could be achieved if they were working in isolation.

5. The organization of the curriculum should allow for unified learning. Experiences that cut across the boundaries of the various subject areas will result in more broadly based learning. Concentration on the development of specific skills, or on specific content, is sometimes required. What is also needed is a balance between specialization and integration, at all grade levels. By nature of their preparation, both elementary teachers and library media specialists are, in terms of subject areas, generalists, though they may have a greater degree of preparation and expertise in a special area of particular interest. This more generalized preparatory background should lend itself easily to the development of effective learning experiences and activities of an integrated nature.

6. The organization of the curriculum should allow for the assimilation of the best information from all sources. As stated earlier, the three basic sources of the curriculum are the students, subject matter, and the society. The need for balance among these three sources was noted. The teacher can provide the best information on the students. The library media specialist can provide the best information on materials and resources to assist in the teaching of selected content. Working together, the teacher and librarian can apply this information to help children eventually become creative contributors to society. A balanced curricular organization will allow for the equal assimilation and application of information from each of the three sources.

Summary

This chapter has provided a broadly based overview of the curriculum planning process. Relationships between the major curriculum components have been examined. Each curricular component affects the others, and a modification in any one component will require corresponding adjustments in the others. The curriculum planning process itself is a dynamic, ongoing one. Effective planning requires at least a basic understanding of how this process works. Although each individual situation will have different influencing factors present, the basic organizing principles and process remain the same for all situations. This includes defining objectives, content, instructional strategies, and evaluation methods.

There are three recognized sources of the curriculum: the learners, the society, and the body of knowledge. Curriculum planners need to be aware of the importance of drawing from each of these sources in a balanced manner when planning and developing curriculum. Three types of learning outcomes have also been discussed. These are new knowledge, values and skills. Long-range learning outcomes should represent a balance among these three areas. Specific learning experiences may place more emphasis on one of these areas, and be one step in a planned sequence of learning experiences resulting in a balanced outcome.

The library media center plays an important role within the larger curriculum planning process. However, the most effective use of the library media center can be realized only through the cooperative planning efforts of the classroom teacher and library media specialist. A comprehensive view of the curriculum planning process includes acknowledgment of use of the library media center as an essential part of that process.

References

Beauchamp, George A. "A Hard Look At Curriculum," *Educational Leadership* 35 (February 1978), pp. 404–409.

Caswell, Hollis, L. "Persistent Curriculum Problems," *The Educational Forum* 63 (November 1978) pp. 99–110.

Doll, Ronald C. *Curriculum Improvement: Decision Making and Process,* 5th ed. Boston: Allyn and Bacon, Inc. 1982.

Oliva, Peter F. *Supervision for Today's Schools.* New York: Thomas Y. Crowell Co., 1976.

Saylor, J. Galen, Alexander, William M., and Lewis, Arthur J. *Curriculum Planning for Better Teaching and Learning.* 4th ed. New York: Holt, Rinehart, and Winston, Inc., 1981.

Shepherd, Gene D., and Ragan, William B. *Modern Elementary Curriculum.* 6th ed. New York: Holt, Rinehart, and Winston, Inc., 1977.

Taba, Hilda. *Curriculum Development: Theory and Practice.* Harcourt, Brace and World, Inc., 1962.

Tanner, Daniel, and Tanner, Laurel N. *Curriculum Development: Theory into Practice.* 2nd ed. New York: Macmillan Publishing Co., Inc., 1980.

Tyler, Ralph W. *Basic Principles of Curriculum and Instruction.* Chicago: The University of Chicago Press, 1949.

Chapter 4

CURRICULUM DESIGN PATTERNS

THE CURRICULUM DESIGNS discussed in this chapter are rarely found operating in their "pure" forms. Most educational programs have drawn elements from several of the more common curriculum designs, and fused them into a plan for a particular situation.

All curriculum designs, no matter how diverse, have certain common organizing elements. These elements arise directly from the planning models discussed in the previous chapter, and help form the basis upon which decisions regarding the curriculum are made. They are broadly based and include the following:

- Consideration and determination of the basic factors relating to the main goals of the plan. This involves an examination of the sources of the curriculum. The study of the nature of the group of learners for whom the plan is being devised, the societal requirements and aims, and the knowledge required to fulfill these needs and aims will provide the planners with necessary data upon which to make decisions regarding the basic design.

- The formulation of broad goals followed by more specific objectives arises from this initial study of basic factors impinging upon the design of the curriculum. Required skills, understandings, attitudes and affects, and abilities are determined.

- The next design element is that of the selection of appropriate learning experiences. The nature of these experiences is determined by the information generated from the first two design considerations. The widest range of experiences possible in a given situation should be considered, but in a systematic manner. The organization of these experiences needs to reflect a logical and hierarchical pattern.

• The other element of any curriculum design is evaluation. Evaluation procedures and techniques need to be determined, both in terms of student progress and curriculum validity.

An additional factor is the actual implementation of the design. What necessary arrangements must be made? What are the actual possibilities within the parameters of the given situation? What logistics in terms of personnel and materials must be worked out for successful implementation of the design? What are the limitations? Space, money, time, availability of certain types of materials?

Flexibility and creativity should be the hallmarks of curriculum design. A solid structure for any plan is essential, but a rigid one can stifle creativity and severely limit learning outcomes. The characteristics, advantages, and disadvantages of six different curriculum designs are delineated in the sections that follow.

The school library media center can be actively incorporated into any of these designs. Though its use may be more extensive in some designs than others, purposeful use of the center will always contribute to the quality of the learning experiences and activities taking place within the design.

The Subject-Centered Design

The subject-centered curriculum design is probably the oldest and most widely known type of curricular design. Its origins can be traced back to the ancient Seven Liberal Arts curriculum of classical Greece and Rome and medieval times.

Characteristics

This curriculum design pattern has a comprehensive orderliness about it; it is based on a relatively simple organizational structure. It tends to be somewhat rigid and compartmentalized, with mastery of subject matter being the central task. Standards, including evaluative ones, are set in terms of the amount of subject matter "covered," and learner mastery of content.

Learning sequences are generally arranged in a step-by-step sequencing pattern. The topics to be covered are defined, as well as the order in which they care to be presented. The textbook is generally used as the primary instructional tool.

The breadth of the subject-centered curriculum is determined by the number of subjects taught. Each subject included within the plan has three characteristics; 1) a unique body of content, 2) its own intellectual discipline (for example, the scientific method, the historical method, etc.), and 3) its own pattern for organizing the content. Objectives in a subject-centered curriculum design are derived from important generalizations found in the field of study, and the intellectual processes inherent in that field.

A good subject-centered curriculum design considers the learners in two ways: their previous educational backgrounds, and their intellectual maturity level. This helps in the selection of content to be mastered, keeping it within the ability levels of the learners. The experiences of the learners are considered, to a point, as an aid in identifying centers of interest for organizational and motivational purposes.

Opportunities for incorporating use of the school library media center into the subject-centered curriculum design are primarily content-oriented. The focus is on the selection and use of specific materials in a single content area. Interrelationships between various subjects are not stressed. Operating under the constraints of this design, the use of the library media center would most likely involve locating the "what" of the subject (information and facts), with less emphasis on the "how's" and "why's." Use of the center in conjunction with the subject-centered design may be more limited and narrow than with other curriculum designs.

Advantages

One of the major advantages of the subject-oriented curriculum design is that of tradition. The pattern, by virtue of its longevity, is a familiar one. It is easy to operate and evaluate from an administrative point of view. Program accountability is assessed through objective testing to determine whether or not the content has been mastered.

The subject-centered curriculum is easily planned and implemented. Textbooks, the primary instructional resource, are generally organized within the subject framework. The precise sequencing of this type of curriculum design allows the entire course of study to be more easily perceived and understood. Also, specific learning outcomes are easily determined, and evaluation techniques can be very structured and precise, making record keeping relatively simple.

Disadvantages

The logical rather than psychological organization of the subject matter often requires teaching a great deal of what may appear to be meaningless information. Memorization and drill are often overemphasized. The logical organization of subject matter may not always be the best organization for effective learning.

Another disadvantage of this design is that it is often characterized by rigidity, detachment from life application, and the experiences, needs, and interests of the students. Often, learning of seemingly unrelated, fragmented information takes place, and the relationships between the various subjects taught is not clear.

When operating within this design framework, attempts to respond to life demands frequently result in simply creating a new subject to be taught, instead of exploring opportunities for strengthening interrelationships. In addition, the knowledge explosion presently being experienced by our society places a severe strain on the limits of the rigid subject-centered curriculum design. The subject-centered curriculum design is essentially autocratic in nature. It does not provide, in any great depth or breadth, for the thinking, selecting, planning, acting, evaluating, and replanning skills that creative, productive members of society need.

Figure 4 illustrates the design concepts of the subject-centered approach. The breadth of this approach is augmented by adding more separate subjects. However, additional components stand alone, and are not inter-connected.

The Broad Fields Design

The broad fields curriculum design represents an effort to overcome the fragmentation and compartmentalization characteristic of

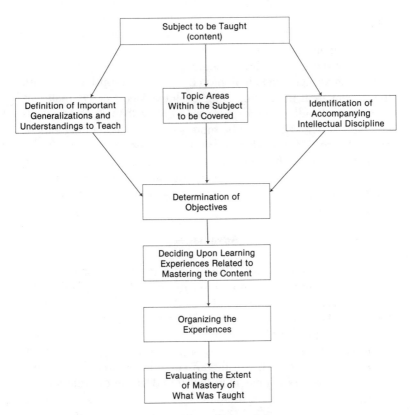

FIG. 4: The Subject-Centered Curriculum Design

the subject-centered design. This is accomplished by combining two or more related subjects into a single broad field of study. The underlying premise is to bring together related subjects around a common area of knowledge. An example familiar to all elementary classroom teachers is the area known as language arts. The separate but related subjects of reading, spelling, writing, speaking, listening, and composition have been combined into one broad area of study.

Characteristics

The broad fields pattern of curriculum design is used widely at the elementary level, and is a significant curricular factor at the secondary level. A greater integration of learning experiences is achieved than with the subject-centered design.

Use of the school library media center within the broad fields curriculum design can help reinforce the interrelationships between the subject areas in the broad field of study. Media center materials and services will be used more extensively than in the subject-centered design. There will be more variety in the learning experiences due to the expanded use of materials and resources.

Though greater flexibility in terms of content is possible using this design, its advantages and disadvantages are essentially the same as for the subject-centered design, but there are several notable differences.

Advantages

The broad fields design allows for greater integration of subject matter, which in turn may contribute to a more functional organization of knowledge. Use of this design also helps in cutting down on the excessive amounts of factual details found in subject-centered designs. The broad fields design is also a more adequate method of organizing subject fields in terms of the problems of living and of learner experiences. This results in content that may be of more significance to the learner than that found in the discrete subject areas.

Disadvantages

This curriculum design still does not provide for integration between the broad fields themselves. Thus, fragmentation still exists, though not as severely as in the subject-centered design. The broad fields design still has a strong tendency to stress content coverage and the acquisition of information at the expense of relevancy to the learner.

One pitfall to avoid when employing this design is the replacement of insignificant details (often found in the subject-centered design) with generalizations that are so broad as to be incomprehensible. This still fails to equip the learner with knowledge of any value, use or meaning. The broad fields design also runs the risk of becoming merely an overview of generalizations which lack depth and offer little opportunity for active inquiry and learning.

Figure 5 illustrates the basic design of a broad fields curriculum construct in the area of general science. Other broad fields (for example, social studies, language arts, fine arts, or health and physical education) are organized separately. As in the subject-centered curriculum design, they are not interconnected.

Social Processes and Life Functions Design

This design represents the direct influence of the society upon the curriculum. Social processes, functions, or problems become

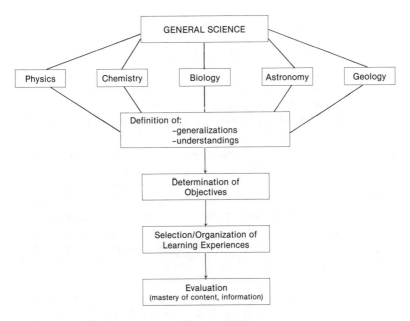

FIG. 5: The Broad Fields Curriculum Design

the focus around which to design and construct the curriculum. "Persistent problems of social living" and the social orientation of the school have been emphasized as important concepts (in terms of curriculum design, organization and structure) since the early part of the century. One way of looking at this particular curriculum design is that it takes social studies and expands it to the point where it becomes the general background of the entire curriculum. Improvement of society through the direct involvement of the schools is a major goal.

Extensive use of the library media center is possible with this design. There are no imposed boundaries present between subject areas. This curriculum design goes beyond emphasis on subject matter alone. Problems, issues and processes become a major portion of the content. Use of the center would go beyond locating factual information. Working out solutions to problems by drawing from many sources would be a typical use of the library media center within the parameters of this curriculum design.

Characteristics

This type of socially focused design is not as sharply delineated as the subject-centered or broad fields designs. Its organizational patterns are based on the study of group life. The curriculum is structured around the various aspects of problems and processes of community life. Because this design departs from the more "structured" nature of the subjects and broad fields, attention must be given to the careful development of continuous themes throughout the curriculum.

Instructional materials for this type of curriculum design may not always be readily available. There is a greater need for locally produced or teacher-developed materials, and probably a greater use of community resources. Expanded methods of record keeping and evaluation are required. While the purpose of evaluation will be to continually assess the validity of the curriculum, methods involving a greater degree of subjectivity than that found in the subject-centered and broad fields designs are required. This not only involves a greater degree of flexibility, but is also more time-consuming than evaluation which is primarily objective in nature. Cooperative planning with the learners occurs to a much greater extent than in the subject-centered and broad fields designs.

Advantages

The skills taught within this type of curriculum design are skills the learners can apply to their everyday living. The learning may also have more immediate meaning to the student. A design of this type provides for larger units of experience, and avoids compartmentalization. A diversity of resources and materials is used in addition to, or in place of, the more traditional textbook. The social problems and life functions design provides an overview of the universal problems of social living. It also provides a basis for learner value orientations.

This design represents an attempt to contribute to the continual improvement of society by striving to meet its needs through better preparation of learners for everyday life.

Disadvantages

Because this design, due to the nature of its content, departs from the more "traditional" designs, special care must be taken in implementing it. A highly structured approach is just as essential, if not more so, in this design as it is in the subject or broad fields design. Accountability is of the utmost importance in the use of this design. The validity of the various methods and materials used may be questioned more often by parents and others. Educators need to be prepared to justify use of this curriculum approach, which may appear more open-ended and less structured than the more traditional and widely used subject-centered designs.

Compartmentalization, which this design attempts to avoid, may occur if aspects of social living are used as organizing centers for units rather than as guiding themes for the selection and organization of learning experiences. Traditional modes of instruction may not be the most effective for this type of design. The use of this design may require some retraining and rethinking on the part of the planners as they devise new and appropriate instructional strategies based on social processes and problems.

Figure 6 shows the various "content" elements to be considered in this design and how they are interrelated. These elements include: communication, transportation of goods and people, freedom of the individual, exploration, production of goods and services, and the distribution of returns of production. Also, education, expression of

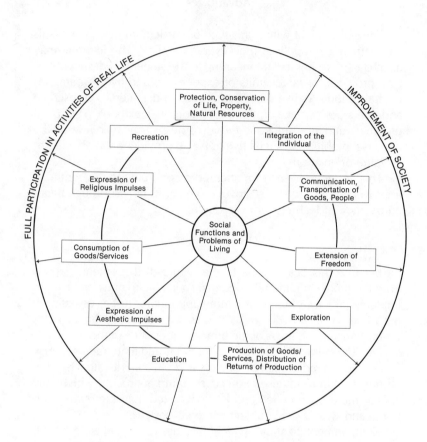

FIG. 6: The Social Processes and Life Functions Curriculum Design

aesthetic impulses, recreation, and protection and conservation of life, property and natural resources. The elements are interrelated, and are collectively known as social processes and problems of living. The ability to function well in each area enables the individual to lead a fuller life, and to contribute to the improvement of society.

The Activities and Experiences Design

This particular curriculum design was devised as one means to counteract the passiveness of learning often found in the subject-oriented designs. It also attempts to compensate for overlooking the needs and interests of the learners, which often occurs in subject-centered designs. The rationale behind this design is that people will truly learn only what they experience. This design has been subject to scrutiny. For example, the question has been raised (Tanner, 1975) as to whether or not this particular design is actually a curriculum design or a teaching method. For purposes of this discussion, it is considered a curriculum design.

A broadly based use of the school library media center is possible in this design. It can become a major vehicle for the "delivery" of the curriculum.

Characteristics

This design focuses on such things as student interests and the integration of content from any subject field. Learning is an active, dynamic process occurring in a natural setting. This may not always be the classroom. Learners are encouraged to use problem-solving skills and methods, and to set their own tasks. Subject matter from many fields is utilized in accordance with particular task requirements. Specific skills and knowledge are acquired on an as-needed basis. The orderly approach to mastery of knowledge or subject matter is not always readily evident in this design.

It is the needs and interests of the learners that determine what will be studied. The course the planning takes is determined, in large part, as these needs and interests arise. This design entails a degree of spontaneity, and skills in the fundamental processes of reading and writing are developed from larger areas of activity rather than as a separate focus.

Advantages

The focus on student needs and interests inherent in this design, when applied to curriculum development in specific situations, can be a helpful *aid* rather than an *organizational center* in the development of units of learning. This will help curriculum workers develop a plan that will incorporate a blend of subject matter and activity, thus providing a better balance. The activities and experiences design emphasizes active learning through such things as manipulation, expression, construction, and dramatization. It also points up that careful attention must be paid to child development sequences and intellectual growth patterns. This has resulted in efforts to consider this kind of information more seriously in any type of curriculum planning and development.

Disadvantages

A major disadvantage of this design is that centering exclusively on the more immediate needs and interests of the learners can result in large gaps in experience. It is more difficult to build a systematic continuity when child-based centers are used as the main organizing principles. In this sense, the activities can become ends rather than means to sequential experiences. There is a certain amount of spontaneity in the planning aspect of this design. This may result in insufficient emphasis on the development of more basic skills, such as in the areas of reading and math.

Figure 7 presents a visual conception of the activities and expe-

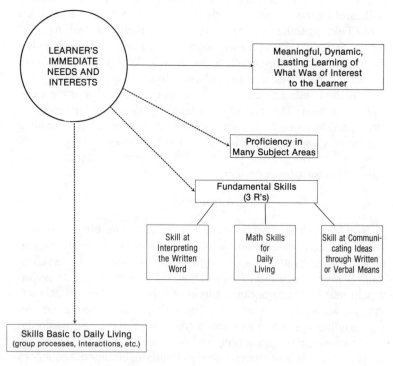

Fig. 7: The Activity or Experience Curriculum Design

riences curriculum design. The learner is not located at the center of the diagram because this is not a well balanced curriculum design. The broken lines in the figure indicate that learning in these areas may not receive consistent attention.

The Core Curriculum Design

The core curriculum design focuses on a set of learning experiences which are felt to be essential for all students. It differs from the subject-centered designs in that its underlying purpose is to create a universal sense of inquiry, discourse, and understanding among learners of different backgrounds and aspirations. A free society is characterized by certain common problems and shared responsibilities. The core curriculum design acknowledges this and is built upon it. It does not take a random approach to planning. Broad areas of concern are examined and sets of learning experiences intended to promote a body of knowledge common to all students are carefully prepared.

A high level of use of the school library media center can take place within this design. There is a better balance between acquiring information and problem solving than is found in some other designs. A wide variety of learning experiences is promoted in the core curriculum design, and the library media center is an essential component in providing them.

Characteristics

A general education is the goal of the core curriculum design. Certain subjects, disciplines, and experiences may comprise the "core" of this design, and the scope can be rather broad. The integration and unification of learning is stressed. This is accomplished through the systematic correlation of subject matter around themes drawn from the contemporary problems of living. Problem solving through reflective thinking is encouraged. Different themes may sometimes be combined. Examples of some possible themes include: civic responsibility, an understanding of economic systems and how people relate to one another within these systems, and family relationships. Also, informed consumerism, development of aesthetic appreciations, and proficiency in spoken and written language may be used as parts of the core areas of learning. The feature common to each of the separate areas mentioned above is that subject matter lines are cut across, and attention is given to the needs of the learner.

Advantages

A major effort is made to relate the core program to life problems and student interests. Problem-solving techniques are used to a greater degree than in some other types of designs. Learners' respect for one another is promoted, and learners have the opportunity to "test out" their own values and ideas. There is an emphasis on cooperative teacher-student planning, and learners are grouped heterogeneously. A wider range of ability levels can be accommodated because the problems being investigated are considered to be universally significant, and students are encouraged to work together and help one another in their problem solving.

Disadvantages

It may sometimes be difficult to rearrange content effectively around new problems or areas of interest. Constant attention must be paid to the systematic planning of the core areas, so that they retain validity and sequence. Those who implement such a design are required to be more generalist than specialist in preparation, although specialists can make valuable contributions to the planning and implementation of this design. In actual practice, the core still appears to be essentially subject-centered. A balanced program of subject matter and learner problems may be more difficult to implement, but is more reflective of the true spirit of the core curriculum design.

Figure 8 represents the philosophical orientation of the core curriculum design. It is a general illustration, and does not represent the more specific subject matter or themes that may comprise the core. Different groups of learners are depicted as they enter the core and take part in the learning experiences that comprise the core. Upon completion of the planned learning program, learners of diverse backgrounds are able to interact with one another based on a set of shared understandings and a sense of shared responsibility toward the good of all.

FIG. 8: The Core Curriculum Design

The Process-Oriented Curriculum Design

This design emphasizes the development of various process skills. These are traits and characteristics to be developed in the learner that will allow him or her to become a mature contributor to society. They also enable the learner to effectively confront and solve problems.

Many of the items listed in the following section can be directly developed through use of the school library media center. Materials, resources and services provided through the library media center can heighten the effects of learning experiences intended to promote such skills as learning on one's own, or creating.

Characteristics

Personal attributes and skills to be developed within this curriculum design include:

a) Working well with others (group interaction)

b) Effective leadership

c) Knowing how to take and follow direction

d) Communicating effectively (verbal and written)

e) Making accurate observations

f) Learning on one's own

g) Making decisions

h) Making good judgments

i) Inventing

j) Forecasting

k) Planning

l) Monitoring the effects of one's own activities

m) Taking corrective action when necessary

n) Creating

o) Initiating

p) Developing a sound value system

q) Having self-confidence

r) Being sensitive to others

Educational experiences within this design are organized so as to provide appropriate experiences for the development of these traits. There is also a greater degree of integration of the thinking, feeling, and behavioral components of learning than in some of the more traditional designs.

Advantages

The development of skills and traits which will serve the learner for a lifetime characterize this design. There is a higher degree of carry-over into everyday living experiences than is perhaps found in other curriculum designs, and a better balance between affective and cognitive considerations. One is not emphasized at the expense of the other, at least not to the degree found in some other designs.

Disadvantages

Planning for the development of process skills and character traits can be difficult. Assessment and evaluation within the framework of this design are not always readily objective. Use of this design requires a reorientation in the thinking of educators, parents, and students. The results of implementation of such a design may not be immediately evident, therefore causing skepticism among parents and the public.

Figure 9 shows how the learner transfers these skills in ever-widening circles from himself, to his schooling, to life as a productive member of society.

Dimensions of Curriculum Design

Six different curriculum designs have been examined. It is noted, in reference to the principles of balance in the curriculum, that none of these designs represents a true balance between all three sources of the curriculum: the learner, the society, and the realm of knowledge. Rather, each tends to focus on only one or two of the sources. As teachers and library media specialists work together on developing curriculum designs, they can draw appropriate elements from various existing designs and add their own as they work to create a balanced design to serve their purposes.

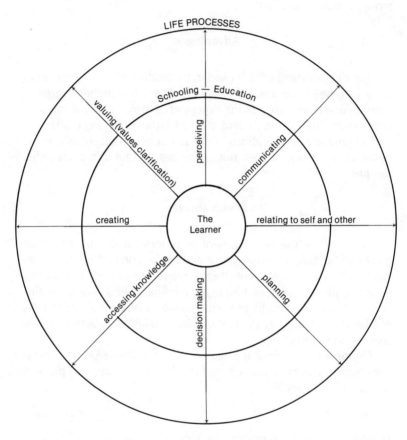

Fig. 9: The Process-Oriented Curriculum Design

However, there is a set of factors that should be present in any well planned curriculum design:

It is possible to identify four process areas which are relatively common to all instructional fields and which should be considered in any curriculum approach. These process or ability areas include: (1) the *language processes* related to the communication and clarification of understandings, personal and social roles, and valuing operations; (2) the *thought processes* which have to do

with verifying and validating data, generalizing, inferring and pre-
dicting consequences (perceptive and creative thinking are included here); (3) the *social processes* through which interpersonal
relationships and actions are promoted; (4) the *abilities* which are
involved in the selection and effective use of educational tools and
resources—people, books, dictionaries, maps, charts, globes, and
the like. Without regard to how the curriculum planning is done,
conscious attention must be paid to how increasing maturity in
each of these four process areas is gained by the learner.[1]

In addition to these factors, consideration must also be given to
the following:

Any over-all curriculum design sufficient to give adequate direction to a program of general education must be considered in
more than one dimension and on more than one operational
level.[2]

Horizontal and vertical organization are the two necessary dimensions to any curriculum design. Horizontal organization
(scope/integration) deals with the side-by-side arrangement of the
components of the curriculum design. Vertical organization (se-
quence/continuity) deals with the longitudinal arrangement of the
design components.

A spiral concept of the curriculum provides for both horizontal
(widening of knowledge) and vertical (deepening of knowledge)
aspects of the curriculum design simultaneously. The well planned
implementation and application of any curriculum design will take
both of these dimensions into account for the heightened sense of
continuity and interrelatedness they provide.

Figure 10 is a visual depiction of the concept of horizontal and
vertical articulation, as it is carried through from preschool to adult
education.

Summary

The curriculum designs presented in this chapter are depicted in
their "pure," theoretical form. The human interpretation (imple-

---

[1]James B. Macdonald, Dan W. Anderson, and Frank B. May, eds., *Strategies of
Curriculum Development: Selected Writings of the Late Virgil E. Herrick* (Columbus,
Ohio: Charles E. Merrill Books, 1965), pp. 8–9.

[2]*Ibid.*, p. 26.

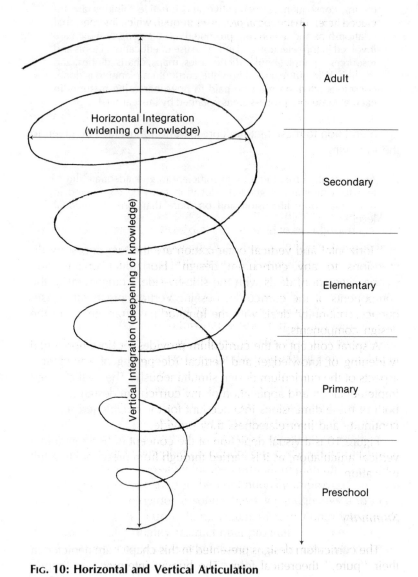

FIG. 10: Horizontal and Vertical Articulation

mentation) of each design would result in the designs varying somewhat from setting to setting. Also, curriculum planners (teachers
and librarians) may draw elements from several of these designs to
create one especially suited to their situation. Knowledge of these
basic designs will allow teachers and library media specialists a
wider range of planning options to choose from or combine.

A number of planning options and considerations will also allow for the creation of a more balanced curriculum plan. A balanced plan, as it makes use of elements from the various curriculum
designs, is needed in order to provide experiences addressing the
cognitive, affective, and psychomotor aspects of learning. Balance
in the plan will result from careful attention to the learners themselves, problems in the larger society, and knowledge the learner
needs.

Teachers and librarians must be able to see beyond their immediate situation when planning and designing curriculum. The plan
they develop must properly sequence with the larger school plan,
and must also integrate with other plans being implemented for the
same group of learners concurrently.

References

Doll, Ronald C. *Curriculum Improvement: Decision Making and
    Process.* 5th ed. Boston: Allyn and Bacon, Inc., 1982.

Herrick, Virgil E., Goodlad, John, Estvan, Frank, and Eberman,
    Paul W. *The Elementary School.* Englewood Cliffs, N.J.:
    Prentice-Hall, Inc., 1956.

Herrick, Virgil E., and Tyler, Ralph W., eds. *Toward Improved
    Curriculum Theory.* Chicago: The University of Chicago
    Press, 1950.

Macdonald, James B., Anderson, Dan W., and May, Frank B., eds.
    *Strategies of Curriculum Development: Selected Writings of
    the Late Virgil E. Herrick.* Columbus, Ohio: Charles E. Mer-
    rill Books, Inc., 1965.

Saylor, J. Galen, Alexander, William M., and Lewis, Arthur J. *Curriculum Planning for Better Teaching and Learning*. 4th ed. New York: Holt, Rinehart, and Winston, Inc., 1981.

Shepherd, Gene D., and Ragan, William B. *Modern Elementary Curriculum*. 6th ed. New York: Holt, Rinehart, and Winston, Inc., 1977.

Taba, Hilda. *Curriculum Development: Theory and Practice*. Harcourt, Brace, and World, Inc., 1962.

Tanner, Daniel, and Tanner, Laurel N. *Curriculum Development: Theory into Practice*. New York: Macmillan Publishing Co., Inc., 1975.

Tyler, Ralph W., Gagne, Robert M., and Scriven, Michael, eds. *Perspectives of Curriculum Evaluation*. AERA Monograph Series on Curriculum Evaluation. Chicago: Rand McNally and Co., 1967.

Zais, Robert S. *Curriculum: Principles and Foundations*. New York: Thomas Y. Crowell Company, 1976.

Chapter 5

THE SCHOOL LIBRARY MEDIA CENTER AS AN ACTIVE, CENTRAL FORCE IN THE CURRICULUM

Underlying Principles

THE SCHOOL LIBRARY media center has traditionally been perceived as ancillary to the instructional program (curriculum) of the school. Yet, the professional literature repeatedly stresses the importance of the library media center as an integral part of the total school curriculum. This chapter explores the concept of the school library media center playing a more central role in curriculum planning, development, implementation and evaluation. Using Taba's seven-step model for curriculum planning as the basis for discussion, active use of the media center within this larger planning framework is examined.

Figure 11 indicates the point at which use of the library media center most often appears to enter into the entire curriculum planning process, if at all. Sporadic use of the center occurs when students are required to use it only as part of a special assignment or activity. As can be seen from Figure 11, this results in a very unbalanced approach to curriculum planning incorporating use of the center.

In this approach, the library media specialist generally has little or no knowledge of the teacher's plan. The librarian was not involved in developing the plan, only incidentally in its implementation, and has no input in the evaluation of use of selected materials and resources, or of the plan itself.

Removal of the library media center component from Figure 11 would not affect the remaining components of curriculum planning. The use of the media center is shown only as an added attach-

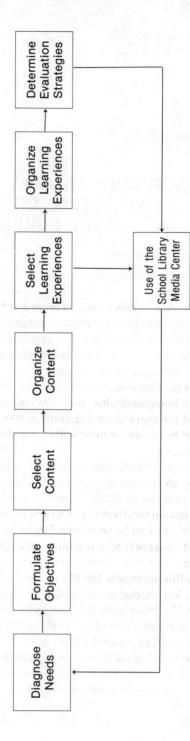

Fig. 11: The Point at Which Incidental Use of the School Library Media Center Generally Occurs

ment, not always needed or used. Unfortunately, it is this type of limited use of the center that very often occurs.

Ideally, the use of the school library media center should be such an integral part of the total curriculum planning structure that to remove it would cause the entire structure to collapse. Figure 12 depicts this ideal, optimum use of the center, incorporating it in an integral way into the entire curriculum planning process. If the media center component of the plan were to be removed, the total curriculum planning process as shown here would be weakened considerably.

This ideal can be achieved only over a period of time, and requires the cooperation of all involved in the planning process: teachers, library media specialists, administrators and supervisors. In some instances it may require in-servicing staff. However, the best way to promote the achievement of this ideal is to prepare educators in the use of this concept in their pre-service programs.

In order to successfully design, plan, and implement curriculum, there are certain principles which must be followed. There is an underlying assumption that the principles are applied in the

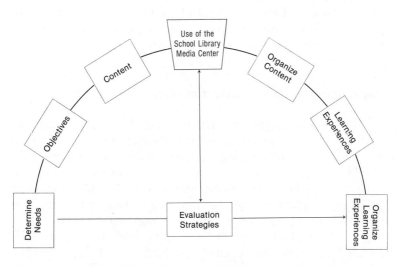

Fig. 12: Use of the School Library Media Center as an Integral Component of the Curriculum Planning Process

context of a cooperative planning effort by library media specialists and teachers. These general principles are: 1) clarification of goals and objectives, and establishment of priorities, 2) analysis and description of learner characteristics, 3) analysis and description of curriculum content, 4) determination of the teaching-learning strategies to be used, and the sequencing of the learning tasks and experiences, 5) selection of suitable media formats and resources to help deliver instruction, and 6) evaluation and modification of each component of the plan or design as needed, based on the outcomes of implementation.

Teachers and librarians by themselves are familiar with these design steps and principles. Teachers use them to develop units and courses of study for their students, and librarians use them to develop units and courses of study for *their* students. Because the teachers and librarians are usually serving the same group(s) of students, combining their planning efforts will result in a more comprehensive, integrated program. Teachers know their subject matter and their students better than anyone else. The library media specialist knows the broadest range of materials and media formats best. Teachers and library media specialists need to work together in order to make the best match between students and materials. This will also help in avoiding unintentional overlap and fragmentation in the total school program. Students will have more frequent opportunities to discover and understand interrelationships between various learning experiences and concepts.

Approaches to Cooperative Planning

In the planning effort, the librarian must be involved from the start. What often happens is that the librarian is not brought into the process (if at all) until the learning activities are implemented. The library media specialist is often expected to produce needed materials on either short notice or no notice at all. A planning effort involving the librarian from the beginning will expand the base of possible learning experiences, and corresponding use of the media center. This will allow the librarian to be familiar with the "big picture." Learning activities can be planned sequentially, as there is a larger context to draw from in their preparation. The solution to this dilemma lies not in "getting the teachers to use the library," but rather in helping them reconsider some of the ways in which they plan and teach.

A necessary part of a unified teacher/librarian planning effort is the development of a school-wide, K-12 library media skills curriculum. This provides a solid basis for a common core of media center use by all students, and is an essential part of the total school curricular structure. Such a program, developed within this context, will be easily integrated with all content areas addressed within the total school program.

Cooperative teamwork between teacher and librarian can take several forms. Ming (1983) identifies three:

1) The teacher-planned approach. In this approach, the school library media specialist is a member of the planning team and is consulted regarding available materials and production techniques. The library media specialist may conduct activities in the library that are related to classroom work. These activities are planned cooperatively. The teacher is responsible for the teaching and evaluation of the rest of the unit.

2) The librarian-planned approach. In this approach, teachers are members of the planning and teaching team, but the school library media specialist has major responsibility for the direction of the planned unit.

3) The unified team approach. In this approach, the teacher(s) and library media specialist share equal responsibility and input for the planning, implementation, and evaluation of a course or unit of study.

There are several specific advantages that the third approach has over the first two. One is that teaming helps to build a good working relationship and establish open lines of communication between the library and the classroom. Another is that it ensures that goals are clearly set and understood by everyone. An additional advantage is that it is a sure way for teachers involved in the planning effort to become more familiar with library media center resources and services. It also allows for increased flexibility in dealing with students on an individualized basis.

Role of the Teacher and Library Media Specialist

Teachers and library media specialists each need to have a clear understanding of the role of the other in the instructional program. The role of the teacher involves planning and implementing classroom learning activities with a specific purpose in mind, and also taking part in the planning and implementation of the larger, all-school program. The teacher is responsible for decisions about the learning of a specific group of students. The teacher is also responsible for certain content areas, and is obliged to see that the class attain certain, predetermined goals and objectives within a defined time frame. The teacher is responsible for the organization and delivery of learning experiences designed to achieve these goals and objectives.

The work of the teacher, however, is not done in isolation. It relates to previous learning experiences the students have had with other teachers, and should provide logical sequencing into future learning experiences with other teachers. In other words, the teacher must be aware of both what preceded and what will follow the portion of the total school program within which the teacher is working. The learning experiences of the students can be greatly enhanced and expanded depending on how familiar the teacher is with media center resources and services, and how closely the teacher works with the library media specialist in the planning and implementation of these experiences.

The role of the library media specialist is much more extensive than many teachers realize. Unfortunately, the school librarian has long suffered from being stereotyped as "keeper of the books." However, today's library media specialist is responsible for far more than the acquisition and cataloging of materials. The library media specialist is part of the teaching staff, and is in contact with students on a regular basis. The librarian must be familiar with the total school program in order to be able to search out and acquire the materials and resources best suited to the program.

The librarian is responsible for communicating to the teachers what types of services and materials are available through the media center. Ideally, the library media specialist is also an active member of the various curriculum planning teams operating in the school or district, be they for a particular subject area, grade level, or work with individual teachers on smaller units of study.

In order to clarify further the roles of the classroom teacher and the library media specialist, job descriptions for each position are provided.* Areas of responsibility which would most likely allow for teacher/librarian teamwork are shown in bold type.

CLASSROOM TEACHER
Job Description

Under the supervision of the designated building principal, the classroom teacher's primary responsibility is teaching students assigned to him in the instructional areas as determined by the administration.

This job shall include, but not be limited to, the following:

1. **Initiates, manages, directs, and takes charge of the learning situations established for the students.**

2. **Adjusts the existing District programs to better meet the differing needs of individual students.**

3. **Explains, clarifies, and shows the "what, why, and how" of program components to the students.**

4. Sets a climate conducive to learning based upon the intellectual, physical, social, emotional, and psychological needs of the students.

5. Stresses the development of superior skills of communication and reasoning which assist each student in adapting to a full and productive life in society.

6. Develops within students coping skills which are conducive to both group and individual living.

7. Fosters a learning atmosphere which assists the student to understand and accept himself as an individual thereby helping the student to develop and express an awareness of his own ideas, feelings, values, and needs in a meaningful way.

*Used with the permission of the Fredonia Central School District, Fredonia, New York.

8. **Assists in identifying difficulties found in the learning process for individual students.**

9. **Involves other school personnel on a need basis to assist him with improving his job duties.**

10. Keeps students and their parents sufficiently up-to-date on the students' progress on a regular basis through reports, conferences, phone calls, and letters.

11. Maintains adequate written records and assures their confidentiality.

12. Assumes primary responsibility for the management and behavior of students under his immediate supervision and assists with the general management and behavior of other students as needed throughout the District.

13. Assumes responsibility for the management of areas, supplies, materials, and equipment assigned to him.

14. Assists in the preparing, receiving, and following through of budget requests.

15. **Participates in grade level/department, unit, and committee meetings to actively assist in improving the programs and services of the District.**

16. Submits written and oral reports as requested by the administration.

17. Participates in ongoing professional self-growth such as through reading, participation in District committees, membership in professional organizations, inservice, and/or graduate work.

18. Performs such other tasks as required by the administration.

DISTRICT LIBRARIAN
Job Description

The major responsibilities of the District Librarian are instruction, curriculum, supervision and coordination of K-12 library and media service. In addition, the District Librarian is responsible for: assisting teachers; evaluation of the library and media service staff; maintenance of a regularly scheduled instructional program; and budgeting.

The District Librarian must demonstrate initiative, planning and communication skills, strong leadership, organizational skills, a strong background in instruction and the ability to motivate students to read and learn research skills. The District Librarian must maintain a cooperative working relationship with faculty and members of the library staff.

The District Librarian must demonstrate knowledge of the current principles and practices of library media services, library organization, procedures and policies. The District Librarian takes major responsibility for the growth and modernization of the library and media service in a planned, ongoing program of improvement.

This job shall include, but not be limited to, the following:

1. **Establishes, coordinates, administers and evaluates the library and media instructional program.**

2. **Teaches library and research skills to students.**

3. **Develops a library skills curriculum based on State guidelines and assists teachers in including library skills in the curriculum.**

4. Supervises the Library Media Specialist, Library Teaching Assistant, clerks and audio-visual staff.

5. Supervises services provided for students and staff, such as the loan of books, software, audio-visual equipment and the operation of the television distribution system.

6. **Serves as a consultant to other instructional leaders.**

7. Aids in the hiring of new library and audiovisual personnel.

8. Supplies statistical data (such as circulation and inventory figures) to the Assistant to the Superintendent and prepares reports as required.

9. **Provides leadership, including the annual setting, completion and evaluation of educational goals and objectives.**

10. **Participates in District curriculum development and the development of innovative programs.**

11. **Participates in teacher curriculum planning.**

12. Cooperates and consults with area and regional media directors.

13. Represents the library media department on various District committees such as the Curriculum Council and Professional Development Committee.

14. Participates in County and State professional associations as the District Librarian deems appropriate.

15. Maintains an effective working relationship with building and District reading specialists.

16. **Provides services and media to support the curriculum (through the Audio-Visual Center).**

17. **Instructs students and staff in the use of audio-visual and production equipment.**

18. **Conducts workshops to instruct school staff in the creative and innovative uses of various types of instructional resources and to introduce new library materials.**

19. **Provides reference services to school staff.**

20. **Provides guidance in the selection of reading materials and referral services to individuals and groups.**

21. Upgrades professional skills on a regular basis.

22. **Informs and encourages the staff to utilize available local and regional media resources.**

23. Periodically publishes a newsletter to keep staff informed on media center activities and acquisitions.

24. Annually prepares and presents to the Board the long–range plan for library and media services.

25. Prepares and supervises the library/media center budget.

26. Supervises additions to and maintenance of the book and magazine collection.

27. Fulfills all the responsibilities of an Instructional Leader.

28. Performs other tasks as required by his supervisors.

The responsibilities of an Instructional Leader* are listed below:

INSTRUCTIONAL LEADER
Job Description

Instructional Leader is the term used to designate persons holding a title such as Cluster Leader, Head Teacher, Department Chairperson, Director or Building Leader.

The Instructional Leader works closely with the building principal(s), assigned administrator(s) and/or superintendent. The Instructional Leader is responsible for developing and maintaining a quality instructional program in his assigned curricular area. The four areas of primary responsibility are curriculum, planning, communication and budget. The Instructional Leader maintains a cooperative, professional, working relationship with the other members of his instructional group(s), other Instructional Leaders and school administrators.

The Instructional Leader is a line function between the unit members and the building principal(s) in his area of responsibility. The Instructional Leader is responsible for his regular teaching duties.

The duties of this position shall include, but not be limited to, the following:

1. Acts as a liaison between the teachers in his instructional area and the appropriate administrator(s).

2. Schedules meetings, sets the agenda and provides minutes for his instructional group(s).

---

*Used with the permission of the Fredonia Central School District, Fredonia, New York.

3. Coordinates and assists unit members in preparing budget requests.

4. Supervises inventories of supplies, materials, and equipment in his instructional area.

5. Represents the members of his instructional unit at the Curriculum Council.

6. Coordinates the review of new materials, textbooks, and equipment for his instructional area.

7. Advises the appropriate administrators regarding teacher assignments and class scheduling to achieve maximum staff utilization.

8. Advises the appropriate administrator(s) on the student grouping(s) and/or course prerequisites within his instructional area.

9. Works with his instructional staff, other Instructional Leaders and the administration to achieve structural integrity in the district's curriculum scope and sequence.

10. Collaborates with other Instructional Leaders, administrators, and instructional staff in development, improvement, and coordination of curriculum in his curricular area.

11. Submits reports, as requested and needed, concerning his instructional area, including recommendations for needed changes and improvements.

12. Shares responsibility for in-service improvement and orientation of staff members in his instructional area.

13. Encourages instructional area members to keep abreast of developments in their field through membership in professional organizations, attendance at conferences and workshops, and course work and reading.

14. Occasionally the Instructional Leader may be asked to perform other tasks related to the four areas of primary responsibilities.

Communication and Teamwork

Both teacher and librarian are responsible for the planning, implementation, and delivery of the curriculum. Each brings his or her own particular strengths to the development of the program. Teachers and librarians, drawing on their knowledge of curriculum design, can use this as their common ground for communication (Talmage, 1980). Based on this common foundation, each one supplies the other with information vital in the construction of a solid program of instruction. Instructional "gaps" are filled this way. The key is communication between classroom teacher and library media specialist, starting with the mutual curriculum design language, and complementing it with their own specialties. Figure 13 illustrates this.

The process illustrated in Figure 13 is ongoing. Portteus states: "Interweaving media and curriculum is a continuous process of communication and study."[1] The substance of this communication between teacher and librarian arises from the study of the instructional program. However, certain barriers may exist which block communication. Many teachers are protective of their autonomy and do not want to lose "control" over their students or classroom. The underlying purpose of cooperative planning and teaching is for the improvement of instruction. It is intended, through mutual agreement on the part of both the teacher and librarian, to help each do a better job and provide a strengthened instructional program for the students.

It often falls to the librarian to initiate the effort to overcome the barriers to communication. A demonstration of willingness and competence in a teaching situation will lend credibility to the library media specialist's promoting of integration of the center with the classroom. Another approach is for the librarian to seek out one or two teachers initially, and work with those individuals on the planning and implementation of a unit of study. This can generate a "ripple effect" as evidence of the success of the team effort accumulates. Other teachers will gradually be drawn into trying the same approach.

The cooperative planning issue, however, is not the sole consid-

---

[1]Elnora M. Portteus, "A Practical Look at Media Supervision and Curriculum," *School Media Quarterly* 7 (Spring 1979), p. 211.

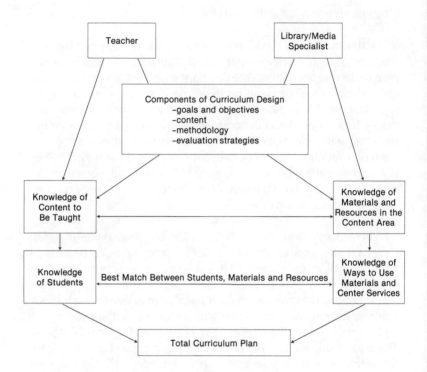

ELEMENTS OF TEACHER AND LIBRARIAN INTERACTION

FIG. 13: Elements of Teacher and Librarian Interaction

eration in the development of a successful teacher/librarian planning and teaching team. Blair identifies seven other factors that
have a direct bearing on the development of a cooperative working
relationship. These include in-service programs provided by the
library media specialist; instructional programs of the school; professional and personal attributes of the library media specialist;
administrative policies; physical facilities and media center climate; teacher attitudes, background and interests; and the extent to
which the media center collection is cooperatively selected and
evaluated.[2]

---

[2]Shirley Blair, "Teachers and the School Resource Centre," *Canadian Library
Journal* 35 (April 1978), pp. 93–100.

A) In-service programs should be carefully designed to introduce teachers to new materials, resources and services that can improve and enhance the instructional program.

B) A well developed library media instructional program as a part of the total school program, which touches every classroom, is a useful tool in encouraging increased use of the center by the teacher.

C) Both the professional and personal attributes of the library media specialist influence teacher willingness to consider cooperative planning ventures. The successful library media specialist is skilled in teaching techniques and materials, works well with others, and is highly visible in the school. Teachers must have confidence that the library media specialist can make a worthwhile contribution to the instructional program, and play a strong supporting role. Teachers must also have enough confidence in their own abilities to allow the library media specialist to visit their own classrooms from time to time, as the instructional program warrants.

D) Administrative policies regarding the use of the library media center by the students can also make a significant contribution to the success (or lack of it) of a cooperative curriculum planning approach. A good curriculum plan may not be able to get past the barriers of restricted student use of the media center. However, policies regarding use of the center should be considered in light of the total school structure, and the curriculum plan adapted as necessary.

E) The facility in which the media center is housed can be a major determining factor regarding the level of its use. An inviting atmosphere and a comfortable setting are important. A well organized, clearly marked collection that is easy to access can also influence the level of use of the library media center.

F) Teacher attitudes toward the library media center are influenced by any training the teacher may have had, and also by past experience in using the center. Teachers often do not receive any formal training in the use of the center in their professional preparation. An occasional in-service program can be helpful, but may not be enough to effect lasting change. Teacher attitudes also have a direct influence on the level of student use of the library media center.

G) The collection itself must also be considered. Teachers need to have a working knowledge of how to select and evaluate collection materials, both print and non-print. Working cooperatively with the library media specialist in this venture will help increase teacher familiarity with the collection, a sense of "ownership," and consequent use of the collection.

The factors discussed above are indicative of the types of problems that may be encountered in a cooperative planning venture. They are presented here as an aid in identifying elements in individual situations that may detract from the success of the planning effort. If the cooperative curriculum planning approach is tried and fails, considerations such as those noted above, or a combination of them, may have been contributing factors. Also, examining each of these considerations *before* undertaking a full-fledged planning effort may point up potential obstacles to the success of the plan. Appropriate strategies can then be devised. Use of the team approach may generate more creative solutions to problems encountered in the planning and implementation process.

Planning Considerations

Problems can be prevented from becoming major obstacles if they can be anticipated before they occur, and strategies devised to overcome them. Erikson has suggested five guiding principles that can be helpful in this type of planning:[3]

---

[3]Carlton W. H. Erikson, *Administering Instructional Media Programs* (New York: Macmillan Co., 1968), pp. 113–115.

1. The selection of materials is based on a valid (educational) purpose, and the needs of the group of students being served.

2. The teacher and library media specialist take into account the development of learner readiness for use of various media formats.

3. Details for the physical arrangements for use of various media formats are worked out ahead of time. This will maximize learning time and focus learner attention on content, not equipment set-up.

4. The teacher and library media specialist will provide the guidance necessary for appropriate learner action and reaction as a result of the use of various media formats.

5. The teaching strategies and accompanying media and materials used to help implement the strategies should be subject to continual evaluation.

These guidelines should also be a useful tool in ensuring that media use is based on curricular needs, and is not a function of what happens to be handily available in the media center. Instructional direction is determined by established objectives, not by available materials.

A Sample Curriculum Plan

A sample curriculum plan is presented as an example of one way to construct a written plan. For purposes of this discussion, it will be assumed that a needs assessment has already been conducted. Following the needs assessment, a short statement of rationale is developed. This is followed by a statement of the broad goals and objectives of the plan. Content is then determined, based on the objectives. Suggested methodology for conveying the content is outlined. This is complemented by a materials and resource list of available, appropriate instructional media. Information on how both learner progress and the quality of the plan itself will be evaluated is included.

Written curriculum plans as developed by different groups may vary in appearance. However, the basic elements of curriculum design are included in any plan: goals and objectives, content, methodology, and evaluation strategies.

LIBRARY MEDIA SKILLS CURRICULUM
GRADE 5

Rationale for the Plan

The acquisition of skills in the use of the library media center and its materials is important for several reasons. Children need to know where and how to access information in order to solve a learning problem, and also for personal use and enjoyment. These skills, developed within the school setting, can also be applied outside of the school setting in any library or center for learning. The skills encompassed in this curriculum plan have both immediate and future applicability.

Classroom instruction can be broadened considerably through the integration of this plan with all subject areas. Learning and applying these skills lends itself to more successful independent work. Children will know *how* to start and successfully complete an independent project. This is directly related to individualization of instruction.

In order for this plan to reach its greatest level of effectiveness, it must be interwoven into the entire instructional program. Teaching these skills in isolation reduces their meaning, and students will not readily see the connection between these skills and the rest of their education. Therefore, they should always be presented within the context of learning taking place in many different content areas. These skills are as effective in mathematics and science as they are in language arts and social studies.

The skills of media center/materials use are the tools for productive thinking, effective learning, and creative problem solving. Thinking, learning, and problem solving require raw materials from which to fashion new ideas, concepts, or products of learning. The library media center, in cooperative conjunction with the classroom, is the obvious place in which to find these raw materials.

Goal of the Plan

The long-range goal of this curriculum plan is for the learner to become an efficient user of libraries and their many types of materials.

Objectives of the Plan

—An understanding of the organization of the library media center, and knowledge of where each of the various types of materials is kept, and how they are arranged. This includes both print and non-print materials.

—Knowledge of how materials in the library media center are classified. This includes familiarity with the Dewey Decimal System.

—An understanding of how the card catalog is arranged, and the ability to be able to interpret accurately the information on the various types of catalog cards.

—Competence in locating and using a variety of resources in the library media center, both print and non-print.

Content Outline

I. *Orientation and Care of Materials*
    — library citizenship
    — location of materials
    — care of library books and other materials
    — reading for pleasure, reading for information
    — circulation procedures

II. *Parts of a Book*
    — cover and spine
    — title page
    — copyright
    — table of contents
    — illustrations
    — preface
    — introduction
    — appendix

— glossary
— bibliography
— index

III. *Card Catalog, Classification and Arrangement*
    — alphabetical order (to the third letter)
    — Dewey Decimal System
    — shelf labels and arrangement
    — relation of call number to location of book (locating books)
    — types of catalog cards; subject, author, title, cross-reference
    — content of card catalog
    — tray labels and guide cards
    — subjects
    — fiction and non-fiction

IV. *Research and Reference Tools*
    A. Dictionaries
        — location
        — alphabetical order
        — guide words, tabs
        — unabridged and abridged
        — appendices
        — use of classroom dictionaries
    B. Encyclopedias
        — location
        — alphabetical order
        — index volume, cross-reference
        — comparisons (between different sets)
    C. Special Reference Materials
        — location and use of atlas, almanac, etc.
        — vertical file materials

V. *Magazines and Readers' Guide*
    — location
    — care in handling
    — circulation policy
    — source of current information
    — scope, important departments
    — *Readers' Guide to Periodical Literature*

VI. *Non-Print Materials*
  — maps (chart and relief) and globes
  — records/record player
  — transparencies/overhead projector
  — filmstrips/filmstrip viewers/filmstrip projectors
  — slides/slide viewers/slide projectors
  — filmstrip/record or filmstrip/tape kits
  — slide/tape kits
  — boxed kits of hands-on materials
  — study prints
  — art prints
  — audio tapes/tape recorder
  — realia
  — computers/software
  — film loops/film loop projectors
  — television/video tapes/VCR units/video cameras
  — films (16mm)/film projectors
  — microfiche/microfilm/microprint readers

Suggested Instructional Methods and Resources

There are many possibilities for instructional strategies. The teacher and library media specialist together determine the most effective strategy or combination of strategies. Some suggested methods are: small group work, classroom presentations, individualized instruction, lectures, demonstrations, field trips, independent study, hands-on experiments, role playing, class discussion, or group projects.

These, or others not mentioned here, may be employed singly or in various combinations to achieve the instructional objective(s). The following set of guidelines for planning instruction [of library media center skills] may be helpful:[4]

  • The skill should be taught in a functional manner, within the context of study.

_____

[4]Eunice Johns and Dorothy McClure Fraser in *Skill Development in Social Studies*, ed. by Helen McCracken Carpenter. Thirty-Third Yearbook. (Washington, D.C.: National Council for the Social Studies, 1963), pp. 311–312.

- Be sure the learner understands the meaning and purpose of the skill, and is motivated to develop it.

- Carefully supervise the learners in their first attempts at applying the skill. Help in forming correct habits from the start. Independence will come later.

- Be prepared to provide individual help (diagnosis and follow-up) for those who may need it.

- Present skill instruction at increasing levels of difficulty. Growth in skills should be cumulative as the learner progresses through school.

- Opportunities for the generalization of the skills learned need to be provided. Applying the skill in many and varied situations will help it to become a permanent part of the student's repertoire.

- Introduce skills as they are needed by the learner. Concurrent development of more than one skill is advantageous to the advancement of learning.

Materials

A list of available materials should be developed to aid in the implementation of the curriculum plan. Such a list should include appropriate books, filmstrips, software, multi-media kits, films and videos, and reference materials for teachers.

Evaluation

Evaluation of the curriculum plan is both formative and summative. Formative evaluation occurs at each step of the planning process. Each part of the plan is compared to the originally stated objectives, and is also evaluated in terms of its appropriateness for the students who will learn from the plan. Formative evaluation is useful in that it helps maintain the proper focus and direction for the plan. Summative evaluation examines the outcomes of the plan, and is useful for determining its merit for other groups of learners.

Questions to ask when evaluating the curriculum plan itself include:

- Was progress evident toward the attainment of the broad goals stated for the plan?

- Were the objectives of the plan met? What is the evidence?

- Was the content "valid"? Was it directly related to the objectives?

- Was the content relevant to the student? Was it directly related to his previous learning experiences?

- Were the needs of the learners met?

- Were the learners interested? Motivated? Did they want to know more? Did they understand the purpose of what they were doing? Were the learning activities organized in a logical, sequential fashion?

- Were the instructional materials and strategies appropriate for the learners? Appropriate to the content?

- What were the strengths of the plan? The weaknesses?

- What modifications or changes need to be made to improve the plan? Why?

Monitoring student progress toward objectives provides an indicator of how successful the chosen instructional strategies are, and whether or not they need to be modified. This is directly tied to use of media center materials and resources. Formative evaluation provides feedback that prevents wasted effort on strategies, methods, and/or materials that do not work well for the students.

Ways of evaluating student progress toward mastering the objectives include these:

- Tests and quizzes

- Observation of changes in student behavior

- Quality of student projects and presentations

- Peer teaching efforts (a student who has mastered the content or a skill can successfully teach it to a classmate)

- Level of student participation in the learning activities

• Level of transference of skills mastered into new learning
  situations

Instructional Design

Once the initial curriculum planning groundwork has been accomplished, the next step becomes more specific. The actual learning experiences and activities are designed and organized sequentially.

The instructional design process mirrors the larger curriculum
planning process, only now the teacher and librarian are operating
within an already established structure. Instructional design involves constructing the smaller building blocks to fill out the larger
curriculum framework. It is a short-range process occurring within
the long-range curriculum planning process. Instructional design is
concerned with specific, immediate outcomes, and is the mecha-
nism that keeps the larger curriculum plan in motion. It is at the
instructional design step that the relationship between curriculum
development and media center services becomes especially clear.

Instructional design can be thought of as a way to solve instructional problems. Sullivan states:

> Instructional design offers alternatives for learning to students and
> alternatives for teaching to faculty. Programs can be designed to
> meet a variety of purposes—enrichment, reinforcement, remedia-
> tion; a variety of grouping patterns—individual, small group,
> large group; a variety of modes—independent study, discussion,
> demonstration. The analysis of each identified problem will pro-
> vide clues to the most appropriate design strategy. The library
> media specialist's involvement with instructional design provides
> yet another means to explore ways to meet diverse learning needs
> and styles.[5]

Instructional design is a means of translating the curriculum
from theory into action. The curriculum plan outlines what will be
accomplished; instructional design determines *how* this will be accomplished. While the initial curriculum plan is outlined only
once, with modifications as needed upon implementation, the in-

---

[5]Janet S. Sullivan, "Initiating Instructional Design into School Library Media
Programs," *School Media Quarterly* 8 (Summer 1980), p. 256.

structional design process is put into motion many times within the larger curriculum framework and is done within the confines of that framework.

Elements of Instructional Design

Elements of instructional design are similar to those of curriculum design, but are addressed in greater detail.

A. Needs Analysis: Clearly define the instructional problem to be addressed (exactly what is the content to be mastered in this instructional sequence) so that specific needs can be identified.

B. State Instructional Objectives: State the objectives in a clear, concise manner, so that both instructor and student know exactly what is expected in terms of outcomes. Include a description of student performance that will indicate attainment of the objectives.

C. Determine Instructional Modes: Determine which mode (or combination of modes) of instruction will best convey the content. Modes of instruction include the following:
- Lecturing
- Discussion (large group, small group)
- Textbook exercises
- Recitation
- Grouping by ability, achievement, or interest
- Questioning
- Discovery
- Inquiry
- Role playing
- Tutoring
- Peer tutoring
- Problem solving
- Oral reports
- Written reports
- Visual reports
- Displays (development of)
- Drill
- Use of audio media
- Use of video media

- Laboratory
- Programmed instruction
- Field trips
- Tests
- Homework
- Independent study
- Demonstrations
- Hands-on experiences
- Simulations
- Games
- Computer assisted instruction
- Manipulation of materials and objects

D. Select Appropriate Media: Select media in line with objectives from the media center collection. Create or adapt materials as needed.

E. Develop Instructional Sequence: Arrange media and materials into a logical sequence to facilitate achievement of the stated objectives.

F. Implement Sequence: Have the students actually engage in the planned activities. Ongoing program evaluation requires that this stage be watched closely and modified as needed.

G. Evaluate Outcomes: Use such things as observations, tests, projects, or reports to determine if the student has met the objective(s). Evaluate the outcomes of student learning as well as the instructional design itself. Did the students attain the objectives? What is the evidence? If they did not, what adjustments need to be made to the instructional design in order for the students to achieve the stated objectives?

Additional considerations when designing instruction are an analysis of learner characteristics and an awareness of any constraints present in the learning environment that would influence the way the design is structured.

An Example of Instructional Design

This instructional design example is derived from the sample curriculum plan presented earlier. The reader should assume that the classroom teacher and library media specialist have conferred on the lesson and its content. This is an example of teaching a library media skill in the context of work the students are doing in the classroom. Specifically, it is a design for teaching 5th grade students how to interpret the information on a catalog card, and is integrated into a classroom science unit on volcanoes.

I. **Statement of need:** Students must know how to interpret the information found on a catalog card in order to be able to locate the information on volcanoes.

II. **Objectives:**

a) The students will correctly identify a catalog card by type: subject, title, author, and also the type of media format it represents.

b) The students will be able to interpret all pertinent information contained on catalog cards for various media formats.

c) The students will successfully locate information on volcanoes as part of a classroom science unit using the three types of catalog cards. (Science unit objectives include understanding how volcanoes are formed, and being able to identify the different parts of a volcano.)

III. **Mode of Instruction:**

a) Large-group lecture in media center using visuals (filmstrips, and transparencies of the three types of catalog cards, with each part labeled.)

b) Individual written follow-up exercises (worksheets to identify the three types of catalog cards: subject, title, author). Label the parts.

c) Small groups assigned to practice locating specific materials (on volcanoes) using the card catalog. This includes books, filmstrips, multi-media kits, study prints, models, films, etc.

d) Individual or small-group review and reinforcement on how to use the card catalog to locate materials in various media formats through use of subject, title, and author cards. This includes use of materials such as filmstrips, software, worksheets and games on using the card catalog to reinforce and broaden the application of this skill.

IV. **Determine learning sequence:** Here is a suggested learning sequence:

a) A motivational session with the librarian, teacher and students. Knowing how to use the card catalog is an important skill in solving problems, finding answers, and clearing up mysteries!

b) Large-group instruction in media center: short lecture with overhead projections.

c) Individual instruction: worksheets on the topic completed by each student, and checked by both teacher and librarian.

d) Small group practice with the card catalog itself. Each group of 2-4 students is given partial information on a specific resource in the media center on volcanoes (for example, the name of the author of a book on volcanoes). The students must record the type of catalog card they used to find the resource, and retrieve the material to take back to the classroom. All work is checked by both teacher and librarian.

e) Review and reinforce use of the card catalog, using various media formats. This takes place both in the media center and the classroom, and can be either large-group or individualized.

V. **Implement instructional sequence:** monitor and adjust strategies as needed throughout the process.

VI. **Evaluate outcomes:** Has student mastered skills needed to use the card catalog? How will you know? Written test or quiz? Correctly completed worksheets? Can the student complete a written exercise on use of the card catalog with at least 90 percent accuracy? Is the student able to locate needed information through use of the catalog at least 90 percent of the time (based on teacher and librarian observation)?

Was the lesson (or lessons) effectively presented? Was student interest and motivation high? Was the material presented clearly, and in a logical sequence? Is there anything that needs to be changed? Instructional mode? Choice of materials? Note: Concurrent evaluation of mastery of science unit skills takes place. Do the students know how volcanoes are formed? Can they describe the parts of a volcano? How will you know? Tests, quizzes, oral or written reports? Construction of models, diagrams?

Summary

A wide range of material has been covered in this chapter. Discussion has moved from concepts that were broadly based to increasingly specific examples. The place of the school library media center within the curriculum planning process has been examined. Emphasis is placed on the continual study of the curriculum in order to ascertain that there is maximum use of the media center in the planning and instructional activities of the school.

This continual study of the curriculum should be undertaken as a team effort by the classroom teacher and library media specialist. Their working relationship is based on the language of curriculum planning and design. Also, there are certain similarities in the defined roles of both teacher and librarian. These areas of similar responsibility form additional links between the work of teacher and librarian in both planning and instruction.

Planning and instructional concerns are addressed in increasing detail as teachers and librarians move from the initial curriculum planning stage into the actual designing of specific instructional episodes and sequences. The function of instructional design lies within the larger curriculum plan.

As classroom teachers and school library media specialists move through the various stages of planning, the effectiveness of their planning can be maintained by basing it on the following principles, sometimes referred to as Krug's four "C's".[6] Effective planning is:

- comprehensive
- cooperative
- concrete
- continuous

---

[6]Edward A. Krug, *Curriculum Planning*. Rev. ed. (New York: Harper and Brothers, Publishers, 1957), p. 328.

These principles apply to curriculum development as well as to
the selection of the most appropriate instructional strategies, materials and resources in light of the curriculum and characteristics of
the learner.

References

Blair, Shirley. "Teachers and the School Resource Center," *Canadi-
    an Library Journal* 35 (April 1978): 93–100.

Chisholm, Margaret E., and Ely, Donald P. *Media Personnel in
    Education: A Competency Approach.* Englewood Cliffs,
    N.J.: Prentice-Hall, Inc., 1976.

Erikson, Carlton W.H. *Administering Instructional Media Programs.*
    New York: The Macmillan Co., 1968.

Haycock, Ken. "Strengthening the Foundations for Teacher Li-
    brarianship," *School Library Media Quarterly* 13 (Spring
    1985): 102–109.

Howlett, Barbara. "Communication Skills and Strategies for Teach-
    er-Librarians," *Emergency Librarian* 11 (Sept.–Oct. 1983):
    14–19.

Johnson, Kerry A. "Instructional Development in Schools: A Pro-
    posed Model," *School Media Quarterly* 9 (Summer 1981):
    256–260.

Klasek, Charles B. *Instructional Media in the Modern School.* Lin-
    coln, Neb.: Professional Educators Publications, Inc., 1972.

Lundin, Roy. "The Teacher-Librarian and Information Skills—An
    Across the Curriculum Approach," *Emergency Librarian* 11
    (Sept.–Oct. 1983): 8–12.

Luskay, Jack R. "Current Trends in School Library Media Centers,"
    Library Trends 31 (Winter 1983): 426–446.

Ming, Marilyn. "Teamwork in the Library—Planning, Teaching, Curriculum Development," *School Library Journal* 29 (February 1983): 40.

Portteus, Elnora M. "A Practical Look at Media Supervision and Curriculum," *School Media Quarterly* 7 (Spring 1979): 204–211.

Shuell, Thomas J., and Lee, Claudia Z. *Learning and Instruction.* Monterey, Calif.: Brooks/Cole Publishing Company, 1976.

Sullivan, Janet S. "Initiating Instructional Design into School Library Media Programs," *School Media Quarterly* 8 (Summer 1980): 251–258.

Taba, Hilda. *Curriculum Development: Theory and Practice.* Harcourt, Brace and World, Inc., 1962.

Talmage, Harriet. "Selecting Non-Print Materials to Best Fit the Curriculum: A Teaching/Learning Center Partnership," *Ohio Media Spectrum* 32 (1980); 4–7.

Tennyson, Carol L., and Tennyson, Robert D. "Evaluation in Curriculum Development," *Educational Technology* 18 (September, 1978): 52–55.

Turner, Philip M., and Naumer, Janet N. "Mapping the Way Toward Instructional Design Consultation by the School Library Media Specialist," *School Library Media Quarterly* 12 (Fall 1983): 29–37.

Chapter 6

THE INTEGRATION OF THE SCHOOL LIBRARY MEDIA CENTER WITH CLASSROOM TEACHING

THE CURRICULUM OF the school is not only a map of what is taught, it is also the map put into motion, and includes all the means used to activate it. This chapter further explores the active integration of library media center services and materials into the entire teaching/learning process.

New media and methods are often "injected" into the curriculum. Library media specialists and teachers must be able to recognize the difference between *injection* of new media or methods into the curriculum, and *integration* of the same into the planned program of instruction. In order to successfully accomplish true integration, certain prerequisites must be met. A thorough knowledge of both the total school program and the library media skills curriculum is required of those involved in the planning process.

Responsibilities of the Teacher

The responsibilities of the classroom teacher in regard to curriculum planning and implementation integrating use of library media center services and resources include the following:

A. A comprehensive knowledge of the content to be taught.

If a science unit on weather is being planned, it is the teacher's responsibility to be thoroughly familiar with all the technical knowledge required for the successful teaching of the unit. Wind patterns, cloud formations and their meanings, effects of temperature, dryness and moisture, potential dangers present under certain conditions, etc. are all examples of knowledge the teacher must have in order to teach a unit on this topic. It will likely require an investment by the teacher of time for research and study in order to become familiar with all the necessary information.

Information is presented at an appropriate level of difficulty for the grade level. For purposes of this discussion, a unit on weather for third grade students is used as the example.

B. An awareness of the types of learning experiences students should have in order to make the learning as meaningful as possible.

A unit such as this presents many possibilities for creative learning experiences. A thunderstorm is something almost all students have experienced, but few probably know exactly what causes one. The teacher could choose to lecture on the topic, but this would probably be the least effective manner in which to convey the dynamics of a thunderstorm.

Cooperative planning with the library media specialist will undoubtedly result in more varied approaches to instruction for the unit. Resource books, films, filmstrips, audio-visual media, kits, and visuals (study prints, for example) will make the learning more meaningful. A field trip to a weather station, if possible, or a guest presentation by a local meteorologist would provide the students with an exciting learning experience. (Principles of career education may also be integrated here.)

There are many simple experiments that can be easily conducted in the classroom. An example of one is the construction and use of a simple barometer as an aid in forecasting the weather.

C. A general knowledge of the materials and resources locally available. Also, familiarity with sources of information for keeping up-to-date on new materials, resources, and methods.

Included here are professional publications, catalogs from publishing companies, *a working knowledge of the school library media center collection,* and the school library media specialist as an additional resource for ideas and suggestions for materials of which the classroom teacher may not be aware.

Responsibilities of the Library Media Specialist

Just as the classroom teacher has certain responsibilities regarding teaching and use of the library media center, so also does the library media specialist. These interlock with the general responsibilities listed above. As the unit is being planned, particular attention is paid to the role of the library media center in its development and implementation, and ways in which use of the center will meet the instructional needs of the teacher, the class, and the individual student. Responsibilities of the librarian include the following and are directly related to the work of the classroom teacher:

A. An awareness of the instructional objectives for the unit (in this case, a third grade unit on weather). An example would be:

> — The students will be able to recognize three different cloud formations; cumulus, stratus, and cirrus.
> — The students will be able to describe the meaning of each of the three formations.

B. Knowledge of specific content. Based on the objectives used as an example, the librarian knows that the teacher will be teaching the following content:

> I. Types of cloud formations;
> — cumulus
> — stratus
> — cirrus

> II. Meaning of cloud formations;
> — cumulus; thunderstorms
> — stratus; the weather will probably change (rain or snow)
> — cirrus; the weather will probably stay the same

C. The library media specialist knows the objectives of the library media skills curriculum thoroughly. Decisions on appropriate skills to be introduced, reinforced, and/or extended within the context of the weather unit are made. At the third grade level, this can include:

Develop and/or reinforce skills in the location and use of dictionaries and encyclopedias.

Be able to explain what an index is and where it is generally found.

Describe the difference between a table of contents and an index, and when it is most appropriate to use each.

Identify a glossary and explain the kind of information it contains, its arrangement, and where it is found.

Recognize that information may be gained from many sources.

Be able to locate needed resources on the shelves.

Discover that the vertical file contains pamphlets, clippings, and reprints organized by subject.

Coordinate sound and visuals using separate pieces of equipment.

Construct a handmade transparency.

Explain what a cross-reference is and show how to use it.

Describe what a bibliography is and tell two places where it might be found in a book.

Know how to use a reel-to-reel tape recorder.

Demonstrate how to use an index.

Make a filmstrip by drawing directly on the film.

Be able to locate specific periodicals (magazines) for pleasure or research.

Be able to use the card catalog to locate materials and information.

The library media specialist knows which materials available in the collection can make a quality contribution to the implementation of the unit, and how these materials may be modified or adapted as necessary.

D. The library media specialist has worked together with the classroom teacher, and knows what types of teaching/learning strategies will be used within this unit. The teacher and librarian have worked out a daily schedule for the implementation of the unit. This way, the librarian knows when each activity will be taking place, and can plan to have the proper materials ready. Also, the plan indicates *where* each unit activity will be taking place, whether in the classroom, the library media center, or at a location outside the school.

E. The library media specialist knows where and how the future application of library media skills learned or reinforced in the weather unit can be applied in future learning experiences in different units. For example, the skills of locating and using the encyclopedia will be used again in an upcoming social studies unit on our country's government.

Evaluation

The library media specialist and the classroom teacher have worked together on the development of the evaluation procedures used to measure unit learning outcomes, and to evaluate the unit itself. These include such things as student projects, tests, and observations.

Also included is an assessment of the original objectives and instructional methods and materials, with adjustments and modifications made where they are needed to improve the unit.

Examples of possible evaluation formats for both learning outcomes, and for the unit plan itself are shown on pages 102–104.

> *Directions (Figures A and B):*
> Place a check in the appropriate box for each item. Find the average and enter this figure into the "numerical average" space. Use the grading scale to determine the equivalent number grade.
> These forms can be filed in folders, each folder labeled with the objective and accompanying activity for which it was used.

Note:

This is a somewhat subjective evaluation tool, and is only suggested as one means of evaluating student progress. Combining these grades with such things as test and quiz scores, and project grades will help in arriving at a more balanced evaluation of pupil progress.

Grading Scale

5.0–4.7 = A+, or 98–100
4.4–4.6 = A, or 96, 97
4.1–4.3 = A–, or 94, 95
3.7–4.0 = B+, or 92, 93
3.4–3.6 = B, or 90, 91
3.1–3.3 = B–, or 88, 89
2.7–3.0 = C+, or 86, 87
2.4–2.6 = C, or 83–85
2.1–2.3 = C–, or 80–82
1.7–2.0 = D+, or 78, 79
1.4–1.6 = D, or 76, 77
1.1–1.3 = D–, or 75
0.0–1.0 = E, or below 75

Parallel Competencies

In the preceding sections, the overlapping responsibilities of classroom teacher and library media specialist have been examined. Although each as a professional has his or her own separate area of responsibility, these merge at enough common points that they should, ideally, interlock. However, each needs to be aware of the actions of the other in the implementation of the total school curriculum in order to strengthen these links.

There is a single set of competencies that both teachers and librarians need to possess in order to incorporate the use of media center resources and services properly into the instructional program. These competencies, originally identified by Clarke for the library media specialist, are essential for the classroom teacher as well. They are applied in slightly different ways by each profes-

EVALUATION OF LEARNING OUTCOMES

Student Evaluation Form

Name of Student _____

Unit Objective/Activity _____

Performance Criteria _____

Achievement Level

	Low				High
	1	**2**	**3**	**4**	**5**
Overall mastery of objective					
Cognitive aspect: (Did child grasp the technical know-how?)					
Affective aspect: (Was there evidence of personal creativity and interest in what went on?)					
Overall Participation –active? –contribute to activity?					

Additional comments:

Numerical Average _____

Grade_____

This form may also be modified to use in the evaluation of
student projects or presentations.

Name of Student _____

Title of Project_____

Purpose of Project_____

Achievement Level

	Low				High
	1	**2**	**3**	**4**	**5**
Overall quality of project					
Project was well researched and organized					
Visual appeal					
Student's enthusiasm and interest in project					

Additional comments:

Numerical Average _____

Grade_____

Name of Unit _____

Objective _____

_____

Objective was: _____too easy for the students (not challenging enough) _____too difficult _____workable as is _____not clear (needs to be more sharply defined)	Comments:
Correlating instructional activities and materials were: _____appropriate to the objective _____inappropriate to the objective _____too easy (not challenging enough) _____too difficult _____workable as they are _____well organized, motivating _____uninteresting or confusing to the students	Comments:
Students' overall response: _____positive _____negative _____indifferent	Comments:

Modifications and Suggestions:

This evaluation form is suggested as only one means of evaluating each component of the entire unit. It is intended for use as a tool to assist teachers and librarians in the continual improvement of their plan.

sional only to the degree that their positions within the school setting require it. The competencies include:[1]

1. Utilization skills, including familiarity with various strategies for mediated learning.

2. Competence in the appropriate integration of media and curriculum.

3. Competence in the instructional design process.

4. Skill in the preparation and production of media.

5. Skill in managing the learning program.

6. Skill in organizing information (in a variety of formats).

7. Familiarity with various media characteristics (and a good grasp of which characteristics best fit certain learning situations).

8. Competence in research and reference work, to be passed on to students.

9. An awareness of factors involved in selecting and evaluating materials, and the ability to apply these factors to actual practice.

Some of the factors involved in the selection and evaluation of materials include: curricular appropriateness, scholarly authenticity, effectiveness of presentation, pupil interest levels, and the technical quality of the materials being considered.[2]

Media Center Services and Taxonomy

Numerous references have been made to the use of library media center *services*. There are many that teachers can utilize on a regular basis to enhance instruction. The key is knowing what they

[1]Norman F. Clarke, "Library Education in an Era of Media," *Contemporary Education* 41 (November 1969), pp. 63–64.

[2]*School Library Media Standards, 1970* (Maine State Department of Education, August, 1970: ERIC Document Reproduction Service, ED 056 716), p. 9.

are, and then making use of the service or services best suited to a particular instructional situation.

Media production services can be utilized to add efficiency to the instructional process, or to try a creative approach to an instructional problem. Production services range from preparation of transparencies and spirit masters to assistance in the production of student-made films, filmstrips, or videotapes. Slide/tape presentations can be created in-house to meet a certain need, and are far less expensive to produce than the purchase of a commercially prepared package would be. Students and teachers can create their own dioramas, displays, kits, or special learning packages in an area set up and equipped with the necessary materials for such work. The range and extent of these services differ from school to school, as does the size of the library media center budget. However, almost every school can offer at least simple duplicating and transparency services, if not the more sophisticated materials production techniques.

Instructional services cover a wide range. These services should not be requested by a teacher without prior consultation and planning with the librarian regarding their purpose and place in the instructional program. Examples of instructional services that can be provided by the library media specialist include these:

a) Arranging to have supplemental materials on a particular topic sent to the classroom to augment classroom instruction and activities.

b) The introduction of materials (by the librarian) centered around classroom units of work already cooperatively planned.

c) Assistance on student research projects, both individual and group.

d) The teaching and/or reinforcement of library media skills directly related to classroom units of work.

e) Book talks related to classroom work.

f) Bibliographies on selected topics of study compiled by the library media specialist can be provided. Students may then desire to choose items from the list on their own, or with the help of the teacher or librarian.

g) The librarian can provide teachers with information on

new materials added to the collection that may be of interest and value to classroom instruction.

The librarian can also offer **consultation services.** This may be directly related to some aspect of curriculum development. An example of this is a recommendation on one media format over another as the most effective way to present the information. The librarian may also recommend *ways* of using specific materials and equipment to enhance classroom instruction. For example, the librarian may be able to offer suggestions on new, creative ways to make use of the overhead projector. Another service offered is that of assistance in the selection of appropriate media and materials for units of instruction. Again, this cannot be done effectively without prior planning and consultation with the classroom teacher.

There are varying levels of intensity at which these services can be utilized. Loertscher has devised an eleven-level taxonomy of school library media center involvement in the instructional program.[3]

TAXONOMY OF SCHOOL LIBRARY MEDIA CENTER INVOLVEMENT

1. NO INVOLVEMENT: The library media center is bypassed entirely in the learning process.

2. SELF-HELP WAREHOUSE: Facilities and materials are available for the self-starter.

3. INDIVIDUAL REFERENCE ASSISTANCE: Students or teachers request and receive information or specific materials for specific needs.

4. SPONTANEOUS INTERACTION AND GATHERING: Spur-of-the-moment activities and gathering of materials occur with no advance notice to the library media specialist.

---

[3]David Loertscher, "The Second Revolution: A Taxonomy for the 1980's," *Wilson Library Bulletin* 56 (February 1982), p. 421.

5. CURSORY PLANNING: Informal and brief planning with teachers and students for library media center involvement.

6. PLANNED GATHERING: Gathering of materials is done in advance of class projects upon teacher request.

7. EVANGELISTIC OUTREACH: A concerted effort is made to promote the multimedia individualized instruction philosophy.

8. SCHEDULED PLANNING IN THE SUPPORT ROLE: Formal planning is done with a teacher or group of students to supply materials or activities in response to a previously planned unit or project.

9. INSTRUCTIONAL DESIGN, LEVEL I: The library media specialist participates in every step of the development, execution, and evaluation of an instructional unit, but there is still some detachment from the unit.

10. INSTRUCTIONAL DESIGN, LEVEL II: The library media center staff participates in grading students and feels an equal responsibility for their achievement.

11. CURRICULUM DEVELOPMENT: Along with other educators, the library media specialist contributes to the planning, structure and implementation of what is actually taught in the school or district.

Readers interested in a more in-depth treatment of the taxonomy are referred to the following:

Loertscher, Dr. David V. "The School Library Media Center: A New Force in American Education," *Arkansas Libraries* 37 (September 1980): 8–13.

Loertscher, David. "The Second Revolution: A Taxonomy for the 1980s," *Wilson Library Bulletin* 56 (February 1982): 417–421.

Loertscher, David V. "Taxonomy Level 3: Maximum Use of the Reference Collection," *Arkansas Libraries* 37 (September 1980): 19–23.

Stroud, Janet. "Library Media Center Taxonomy: Future Implications," *Wilson Library Bulletin* 56 (February 1982): 428–433.

Stroud, Janet. "Taxonomy Level 10: The Instructional Design Function in the School Library Media Center," *Arkansas Libraries* 37 (September 1980): 32–34.

This book is written in the context of teachers and library media specialists operating at level eleven. In actual practice, many teachers and media center staff are operating only at the lower levels of the taxonomy, for a variety of reasons.

In many situations, the library media center is understaffed, and for this reason alone it is impossible for the librarian to have direct contact with the total teaching staff. Achieving level eleven of the taxonomy in its fullest sense may not be possible under such conditions. However, with modifications to make it more practical in a given situation, it can still serve as the goal to work toward.

The daily class schedule may well be one of the biggest deterrants to operating at higher levels within the taxonomy. Teachers and librarians often literally do not have an opportunity for cooperative curriculum development. Even when teachers do have the opportunity to work on curriculum (usually during the summer), the library media specialist is not always included or consulted at any stage of the planning. This can be attributed to the fact that many teachers are simply not aware of the role the library media specialist can and should be playing in their planning and instruction. It is a source of endless frustration to librarians that nine times out of ten, teachers will wait until the last minute before requesting needed materials. Or worse yet, they do not let the librarian in on the secret at all. It is only when a flood of students arrive at the center, all requesting the same materials, that the library media specialist begins to suspect that something is afoot, and starts to make discrete inquiries as to what is going on. The librarian's response to such a situation is usually, "If only I had known, I could have. . . . "

The taxonomy is provided for readers to use as a reference point from which to evaluate the level of use of the library media center within their own school. It shows both what is and what can be, and outlines a logical way to arrive at the highest levels of functioning. Arriving at level eleven is a slow process that could conceivably take several years to achieve. Working successfully with a few teachers at first can help win over increasing numbers of teachers to the integration of the library media center with their curriculum planning and instructional program. Most librarians *want* to work with teachers on curriculum development, and are frustrated in their attempts when they are either ignored or meet with resistance.

Successful movement upward from one level to the next of the taxonomy is largely dependent upon open channels of communication between teacher and librarian. The taxonomy itself is really a description of the various levels of communication that may occur. Reaching the higher levels of the taxonomy is dependent, in part, on how well the classroom teacher understands the (cooperative) planning and teaching role of the librarian. The teacher also needs to understand the nature of the activities the librarian undertakes to perform this role, and how these activities, particularly the teaching ones, are determined.

Working within higher levels of the taxonomy can provide greater and more varied opportunities for integrating use of the center and its services with classroom activities. However, teachers need to be made *aware* of the possibilities before they can begin to work toward the goal of total integration.

Factors to Consider in Cooperative Planning

At the curriculum development level (level eleven) of the taxonomy of school library media involvement in the instructional program, the library media specialist plays an active role in curriculum planning, development, change, and implementation. The librarian's special knowledge of a wide range of sources, materials, the in-house collection, and characteristics of various media formats, coupled with a broad teaching/learning strategies repertoire, make the librarian a valuable member of the curriculum planning team. At the beginning of the planning stage, while the teacher and librarian are viewing the curriculum from its broadest perspective (before they have reached the point of planning for individual units and lessons), there are some major considerations that should help provide important focal points. These can be useful in providing points of contact between classroom activities and use of the center. Lowrie initially identified these considerations as goals for elementary education that are applicable to the school library media program as well. They can provide the basis for the interlocking of the library media center with the curriculum of the school.

A) A broadening concept of the classroom to include all types of living experiences from the family to the international community.

B) The evaluative use of many sources of information.

C) The use of individual, small group, and class activities to help provide for different types of learning.

D) The acceptance of the learner as he or she is, and provision of materials which take into consideration individual differences.

E) An emphasis on problem-solving processes rather than memorization of facts.

F) An acknowledgment of "persistent life situations" of which all children are aware, and about which their curiosity increases as they mature.

G) The need to develop among learners the understanding that education is a life-long process.[4]

Considerations in the planning process up to this point have been rather broadly based. Although stress has been placed on the importance of considering learner characteristics and outcomes in order that meaningful, appropriate plans may be developed, it is important to give equal consideration to another part of the planning process. This is the selection and evaluation of the media, materials, and resources that will be used as tools in the delivery of the curriculum.

Books are often considered the basic materials of education. Even in an era of rapid technological change, the book still appears

---

[4]Jean Elizabeth Lowrie, *Elementary School Libraries.* (New York: Scarecrow Press, 1961), p. 23.

to be a permanent resident. However, books should be regarded as only *one* kind of media format. Other media can, and should be, as basic as books to the instructional process. They should also be viewed as equal partners with books, not replacements for them.

There are several good reasons to consider use of a variety of media formats as a part of the instructional program. Motivation and increased interest on the part of the student is fostered. Use of a variety of media formats can contribute to a heightened perception of the topic being studied. This strategy can also assist in the building and expansion of concepts related to the topic. When used properly, a variety of media formats can make a significant contribution to the overall quality of instruction.

General Selection and Evaluation Guidelines for Media

Once the initial planning of the curriculum and/or unit of instruction has been completed, the selection and evaluation of media and materials that will best help meet the objectives is undertaken. Specific media choices occur at the instructional design stage, where the teacher and librarian are working with a particular instructional sequence. Essentially, the selection and evaluation process involves making the best match between people and materials.

Certain general guidelines may be helpful in selecting the materials best suited to meeting the objectives. Klasek (1972) points out four general considerations that can be applied to the media selection process. These are practical considerations, student considerations, content considerations and teacher considerations.

Practical considerations have to do with such things as the availability of the material (immediately available, or is there a "wait time" before obtaining it?), the cost (reasonable or prohibitive), and the physical condition of the material (high technical quality, in good repair?). Other practicalities include how the material is designed (simple to use, or unnecessarily complex?), how easily the students can access the material, and the emotional appeal and aesthetic value of the medium.

Considerations involving students are similar to those discussed previously at various planning stages. The materials must "match" the student(s) characteristics, and hold meaning for the student in terms of his or her own learning. Also, the level to which the material actively involves the student should be examined. Those materials which more actively engage the student will reinforce learning to a greater degree than media or materials which only allow the student to be a passive recipient of information.

As teachers and librarians select the media and materials which the students will be using, they do so with a clear idea of the content or topic the material is intended to convey. Selection of a particular medium/material is based on its relevance to the objectives of the curriculum. A careful examination of the material is also made to determine the accuracy of its content. This is directly related to the teacher's responsibility to be thoroughly familiar with the subject matter being presented.

An attractive, well organized, and uncluttered presentation is important. The material presented, whatever the medium, must be accurate and up-to-date. This is not to say that all older materials should be disregarded. They may still be useful, at least in part, for attaining the stated purpose of instruction.

Additional considerations involve the ease with which the teacher, librarian, and/or students can make use of the medium/material. It is important that *all* media and materials *always* be previewed by the teacher and the library media specialist. Materials should be used only with full knowledge of the content of the presentation, and confidence that the content is in keeping with the original purposes of the unit.

The selection of media and materials provides the teacher and librarian with an opportunity to recheck the clarity of their original curricular goals and unit objectives. Difficulty in selecting appropriate media may be an indication that the objectives need further clarification. The library media specialist can offer suitable suggestions on what specific media and materials will best contribute to the objectives only if the objectives themselves are clear.

Teachers should refer often to media and materials source books and catalogs in order to develop an awareness of the range of media available for their purposes. This type of awareness can be an asset in relating certain types of media to specific learning and instructional problems.

Media and materials should be chosen to play a variety of roles in the instructional process. They can introduce a unit, call for student interaction with the media, present information, or assist in providing new learning experiences. The creative use of media and materials also helps create greater student involvement in the learning process.

The preceding paragraphs have focused primarily on examining only the media and materials in the selection and evaluation process. Another basis for selection is the learners; their interests, maturity, previous experience, and level of comprehension all need to be considered when determining the quality and suitability of specific media. The learner response to the selected media and materials will be one indicator of how well chosen or appropriate the materials are. Learner response will also indicate whether or not the objectives have been met. This dual interpretation of learner response will provide valuable information on whether modifications or changes are necessary in either the teaching plan or the selection of media and materials, or both.

The general standards discussed in this section should be helpful to the educator who is becoming involved in media selection and evaluation either for the first time or to a greater degree than before. Increased experience and the constraints of a particular location or teaching/learning situation will enable educators to develop their own, more detailed guidelines. The generalizations in the preceding paragraphs can be applied to any media format, but they can be broken down further into more specific considerations. Erikson has devised a sixteen-item set of selection and evaluation criteria, that fall under the heading "Curriculum Relationships." These criteria are:

1. Will the material be usable in direct relation to a teaching unit? To a specific experience, or problem-solving activity?

2. Is the content to be communicated by the material useful and important? To the pupil? To the community? To society?

3. Will the material make a contribution to major teaching purposes? (Or toward the major goals of the learners?)

4. Does the difficulty level of the teaching purposes (the understandings, abilities, attitudes, and appreciations) demand the help of the material being examined?

5. Will the material be likely to call for vicarious experiencing, thinking, reacting, discussing, studying?

6. Is the content to be communicated presented in terms of problems and activities of the learners? (Logically arranged subject matter may be called for at advanced levels of study.)

7. Will the uses of the material being examined be obvious to teachers?

8. Is content to be presented by the material sufficiently rich in concepts and relationships?

9. Does the material possess appropriate content that facilitates the process of inference? Size? Temperature? Weight? Depth? Distance? Action? Odor? Sound? Color? Lifelikeness? Emotion?

10. Is the material accurate, typical, and up-to-date?

11. Is the kind of material uniquely adapted to the achievement of the desired teaching objective? When media are in programmed format for use in instructional systems, are published try-out results valid and convincing?

12. Is the content in the material in good taste?

13. Is the material likely to be of value for a period of seven to ten years?

14. Could the material be used conveniently within a regular class period?

15. Is the content of the material sufficiently rich in number of examples to warrant sound conclusions? That is, are both sides of an issue explored? If not, is the insufficiency pointed out?

16. If the item duplicates content in material already owned, is it sufficiently superior to warrant supplanting the older item?[5]

The importance and value of using appropriate print and non-print materials in addition to the textbook becomes increasingly

---

[5]Carlton W.H. Erikson, *Administering Instructional Media Programs* (Macmillan Co., 1968), pp. 66–67.

obvious when one seeks to provide a variety of learning experiences to heighten the meaning of the content. Such materials can be use to augment the text, and also to compensate for deficiencies and weak spots in the textbook. Alternative modes of student involvement in learning are provided through the use of a variety of media and materials, and motivation is increased. Also, as the teacher and librarian plan together, there is the opportunity for sharing information on individual student needs, whether for enrichment or remediation. Properly selected media can help provide both.

Relationships between the classroom and the media center are strengthened through regular consultation between the teacher and the library media specialist. Media and materials that complement but do not duplicate each other can be used concurrently in the classroom and the center. This should help students to see more clearly the connection between their classroom work and activities they participate in at the media center.

Based on continual study of the school curriculum by all members of the professional teaching staff, sound decisions can be made regarding the acquisition of new material best suited to the purposes of the curriculum. Continual study of the school curriculum will also help maintain a higher level of use of the library media center as a part of the total school program. Involving school library media staff in work on curriculum problems is one way in which to promote this.

Concurrent with the continual study of the school program there should be an on-going evaluation of the use of the media and materials to ascertain that they fit the curriculum, and that the curriculum is not being structured to "fit" around the materials.

Summary

The classroom teacher has certain responsibilities regarding total integration of the library media center with curriculum planning and teaching. Knowledge of the content and skill in planning and presenting a variety of types of learning experiences are required. The teacher must also have a working knowledge of the library media center collection and the services available.

The library media specialist has similar responsibilities, and is also required to have a working knowledge of the total school program, at least in general terms.

Loertscher's Taxonomy of School Library Media Center Involvement illustrates eleven different levels of media center involvement in the instructional program. The highest level represents total media center involvement in the curriculum planning process. The taxonomy can also be interpreted as a set of steps to take in reaching this level of total involvement. It may take several years to attain level eleven. The taxonomy is placed in the context of participation of all staff. However, it may have to be articulated on an individual classroom teacher-librarian basis at first, and given time to grow to include increasing numbers of teachers.

Once others have had a chance to see the positive effects of total media center integration with the curriculum planning and teaching process, they may be more willing to work up through the different levels of the taxonomy. All lasting changes in educational practice take time to occur, and are most effective if they come about under the "grass roots" approach rather than a mandate handed down by an administrative authority to the teaching professionals.

Cooperative planning by teacher and librarian rests on a set of commonly accepted factors that lend a sense of direction to the overall planning process. These are broadly based, and include the evaluative use of many sources of information and an emphasis on problem-solving processes rather than memorization of facts. Also, the importance of using a variety of media formats as a part of the instructional program must be recognized by both classroom teacher and librarian.

Selection and evaluation guidelines for media involve practical considerations concerning the availability of the materials, cost, technical quality, and how easily they can be used by teachers and students. Other considerations are the relationship of the media to the curriculum itself. Valid reasons for use of media include the deepening and broadening of the learning experience for the student, and contributing to the attainment of stated objectives.

In addition to various planning considerations, the importance of on-going study of the curriculum of the school has been emphasized. The main reasons for this are to ensure that the media center is being utilized in the best possible way, and also to continually improve the outcomes of curriculum planning and teaching.

References

Chisholm, Margaret E., and Ely, Donald P. *Media Personnel in Education: A Competency Approach.* Englewood Cliffs, N.J.: Prentice-Hall, Inc., 1976.

Clarke, Norman F. "Library Education in an Era of Media," *Contemporary Education* 41 (November 1969): 61–66.

Considine, David. "Media, Technology, and Teaching: What's Wrong and Why?" *School Library Media Quarterly* 13 (Summer 1985): 173–182.

Cuban, Larry. *Teachers and Machines: The Classroom Use of Technology Since 1920.* New York and London: Teachers College, Columbia University, 1986.

Dale, Edgar. *Audiovisual Methods in Teaching.* Revised ed. New York: The Dryden Press, 1954.

Eisenberg, Michael. "Curriculum Mapping and Implementation of an Elementary School Library Media Skills Curriculum," *School Library Media Quarterly* 12 (Fall 1984): 411–418.

The Elementary Library Media Skills Curriculum, Grades K-6. The University of the State of New York, The State Education Department, Bureau of School Libraries, Albany, New York 12234, September 1980.

Erikson, Carlton W.H. *Administering Instructional Media Programs.* New York: The Macmillan Co., 1968.

Fetter, Wayne R. "An Evaluation Instrument for Instructional Materials," *Educational Technology* 18 (October 1978): 55–56.

Klasek, Charles B. *Instructional Media in the Modern School.* Lincoln, Neb.: Professional Educators Publications, Inc., 1972.

Loertscher, David. "The Second Revolution: A Taxonomy for the 1980's," *Wilson Library Bulletin* 56 (February 1982): 417–421.

Luskay, Jack R. "Current Trends in School Library Media Centers," *Library Trends* 31 (Winter 1983): 429–446.

Olson, Lowell E., "Unassailable Truth?" *School Library Media Quarterly* 12 (Fall 1983): 53–57.

Talmage, Harriet. "The Textbook as Arbiter of Curriculum and Instruction," *The Elementary School Journal* 73 (October 1972): 20–25.

Chapter 7

APPROPRIATE USE OF MEDIA
AND MATERIALS

ONE OF THE MAJOR themes of this book is cooperation and communication between teacher and librarian. Aside from the general premise of providing children with a rich instructional environment, cooperative work has other advantages and benefits. A dual perspective in the planning process can help maintain a better balance between the broader goals of the plan and the more specific objectives. It is sometimes easy to lose sight of the original goals of the plan when attending to the specific details of individual lesson planning. A team-planning approach can help prevent "tunnel vision," or unintentional digression from the original intent.

Cooperative planning also helps in the formulation of objectives most appropriate for specific grade levels. For example, a third grade teacher has more detailed knowledge of the third grade curriculum than the librarian may have. If objectives in the current library media skills program do not quite match this grade level, the classroom teacher can be of assistance in adjusting them appropriately. The same principle can be applied in reverse. For example, the librarian can assist the teacher in the selection of materials at the correct reading levels for individual students.

" . . . Media have become not merely tools, but the building blocks of a more efficient and interesting learning environment."[1] A block structure stands only if the blocks are placed according to a blueprint or plan. The cooperatively planned curriculum provides the blueprint for instruction. Instructional media are the raw materials from which to construct the learning environment. It must be

---

[1]Walter A. Wittich and Charles F. Schuller, *Instructional Technology: Its Nature and Use*, 6th ed. (New York: Harper and Row, 1979), p. 2.

constructed in such a way that it makes sense and has meaning for the learner.

Media as an Active Element in Instruction

A library media centered approach to instruction extends across all subject areas. It should also act as a link between the various subject areas, helping to clarify relationships and strengthen concepts. In this light, cooperative planning can provide information on the compatibility of the existing curriculum guidelines in current use for all subjects taught. Weak links between the content areas can then be addressed and corrected. This type of careful planning can also result in more careful attention being paid to the development of skills involving the integration of knowledge, and to the making of connections between different areas of study.

Related is the fact that too often, library media skills are taught in isolation from classroom units and activities. Consequently, students are unable to make the connection between the two, and use of the skills is not applied in a consistent and broadening manner. In order to accomplish this, it is necessary to establish clear relationships between classroom work and the use of library media resources and materials. Once again, cooperative planning between teacher and librarian will serve this purpose.

As the librarian works with the classroom teacher and becomes familiar with the subject matter the teacher is dealing with, thorough, annotated subject area curriculum guides showing library media center holdings appropriate to the area of study can be developed. These can serve as handy reference tools, both for the teacher and the students. Students can then select items of particular interest from a materials list for further study, or as a part of class activities. A resource list of this kind is a good start to familiarizing teachers with materials and services available in the center. However, teachers may still need a hands-on introduction to the materials; without a proper initial presentation, many valuable materials may go largely unused. Teachers need to see what the materials are and how they can be used. The extent of teacher familiarity with various media and materials can be a major factor in determining the scope of a student's learning experiences.

Underlying all these guidelines is the understanding that library media skills are the means to clearly identified ends, not the ends themselves. That is why it is so essential that the relationship between the library media skills program and classroom activity is made clear to the student.

Just as the acquisition of library media skills is the means to an end, and not an end in itself, so it is with the use of media in instruction. Properly used, media are the catalytic ingredient in the instructional process. They should serve to promote a desired action or reaction in the learner that would not have occurred without their use. Media provide the connecting link between information and the student. Without media, there would be no (or substantially less) interaction between the student and the information, and no (or substantially less) subsequent changes in the behavior or perception of the student. Figure 14 illustrates this concept.

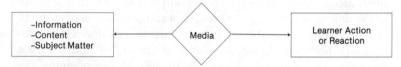

FIG. 14: Media as Catalyst

The concept of media as catalyst does not represent a random interaction of the learner with information. It implies a well orchestrated combination of strategies, people and media intended to bring about a desired outcome. It represents the integration of a specific set of both human and non-human resources. In any instructional situation, one of the roles of the teacher is that of facilitator. The degree of direct involvement with the student will vary, largely depending on the way in which different media are employed in the teaching-learning situation. Paralleling this, one of the roles of the library media specialist calls for assisting " . . . teachers and learners to effectively interact with media to achieve [desired] learning outcomes."[2]

[2]Margaret E. Chisholm and Donald P. Ely, *Media Personnel in Education: A Competency Approach* (Englewood Cliffs, N.J.: Prentice-Hall, Inc., 1976), p. 347.

Evaluating Outcomes

It is interesting to note here that the worth of any particular instructional medium is often measured in terms of student learning outcomes. If there is valid evidence that the objectives were achieved, then the means of achieving them (here, with the assistance of instructional media) are considered to be a valuable and successful part of the instructional process.

However, the *way* in which media and materials are used in instruction also needs to be considered.

- Were the materials used to directly achieve the objectives?

- Was their use timely and appropriate?

- Were they used for valid instructional purposes, or only as a "filler?"

- Did the students see the media as a frill, or an integral part of their instruction?

- Was the medium used only as an attention-getter, for its flash and immediate appeal?

- Do the students recall *what* was presented through the media, or only that some equipment or material that was fun to manipulate was used?

The answers to questions such as these need to be examined carefully in order to determine whether or not the use of the media was valid in serving the purposes of instruction.

Ellington suggests general ways in which media and materials can be used in instruction.[3] These can also be interpreted in the context of evaluating the use of media in instruction. The suggestions include examining use of media from the following standpoints:

- Forming an integral part of the main presentation, showing examples, providing samples to try.

---

[3]Henry Ellington, *Producing Teaching Materials: A Handbook for Teachers and Trainers* (London: Kegan Page Ltd.; and New York: Nichols Publishing Company, 1985), p. 14.

- Providing supplementary material; background information, remedial or enrichment material, providing opportunity for practice.

- Increasing the level of student motivation through use of
  visually appealing, interesting, or "change of pace" material.

- Helping to show the application, relationships, or integration of one topic or idea with another.

These suggestions, as related to the use and evaluation of that
use of media in instruction, go in tandem with the evaluation undertaken in order to determine how well the objectives of the plan
were met. Multiple considerations point up the need to evaluate
media use in instruction in a balanced manner, considering more
than one set of factors. Media use is based on the objectives of the
plan that were originally developed from combining classroom
content area objectives with library media skill objectives. This was
done in order to provide multi-faceted, integrated learning experiences. The evaluation of media use in instruction also needs to be
considered in light of the underlying dual purpose of many of the
objectives; linking the classroom with the library media center to
enhance the learning experience.

Other Considerations

Considering the following will be helpful in ensuring that educational media are used in the proper manner.

The group of learners for whom the medium is intended must be
studied in order to ascertain their special characteristics. This includes determining their general maturity level, the range of abilities of the group (or individual), and the previous experiences the
students may have had with the particular medium or with application of the skill(s) presented.

Know exactly which objectives the medium is assisting the
learners in achieving. *Preview* the medium to determine the appropriateness of its content for the group, and also to judge the quality
of the presentation itself. Materials of poor technical quality may

become more of an obstacle than an asset to learning. They might not be worth the effort.

Instructional "clutter" should be avoided. The use of certain media and materials should reinforce, and be related to, use of other media and materials. Clear goals and objectives should be combined with systematic media selection and evaluation. This will ensure that media are used in a sequentially appropriate instructional manner, and will avoid a jumble of different types of learning experiences in which the connections and relationships are not clear to the learner.

One reason to use media in instruction is to help students develop the skill of learning how to learn. The proper use of media will result in an active learner response. It is through this active response that learning is internalized. It can then be carried over and applied in new learning situations, and added to the student's growing skill repertoire.

Selection of Media

A systematic approach to the selection and use of media helps guarantee its appropriate application in the instructional process. Again, this systematic approach is based on clearly defined goals and objectives. Klasek mentions five guidelines that are useful in ensuring the best use of media and materials based on a set of well-defined objectives.[4]

A. A visual presentation can be of valuable assistance in learning how to actually perform a given task or apply a new skill. Observing learner behavior will provide information on the degree of transfer from a learning situation to actual practice. A high degree of transfer generally indicates that the learning objective(s) have been met.

B. A verbal presentation of facts and concepts may not always be enough. The use of supporting visual materials to assist in the

---

[4]Charles B. Klasek, *Instructional Media in the Modern School* (Lincoln, Nebraska: Professional Educators Publications, Inc., 1972), p. 45.

verbal presentation of information provides cues that the learner is much more likely to internalize. It is one way of taking an abstract verbal representation and making it more concrete so that the student can better relate it to previous experience.

C. Sometimes it is not possible for students to experience *directly* certain learning tasks or concepts. It may by physically impossible to bring certain experiences to the classroom, or for the students to go to places where certain events are actually taking place. It is in situations like this that various media and materials can provide "substitute" learning experiences. They approximate the actual experience as closely as possible, and provide the next best alternative to actually being there.

D. If the teacher wants the learners to be able to see relationships and interrelationships between certain ideas and concepts, the textbook alone may not always be the most effective way in which to convey this type of information. The use of visuals can be a valuable aid in discerning relationships that may not be readily obvious in printed materials.

E. Another consideration has to do with the appeal of a particular medium, and its ability to attract and hold the learner's attention. Care must be exercised here, however, to focus on the objectives as the primary basis for the selection of a particular medium. Even though the ideal use of media is to educate, not entertain, the worth of a particular medium must still be judged, in part, on the basis of its appeal. Just as media must be of high technical quality, they must also be able to attract the attention of the learner without *distracting* him from the objective.

Bender has summarized the appropriate use of media and materials into the "5 R's":[5]

> the *right* material for the
> *right* person at the
> *right* place at the

5David R. Bender. "Networking and School Library Media Programs," *School Library Journal* 26 (November 1979): p. 30.

right time to be used in the
right way.

Effective Use of Media

Effective use of media is a multi-step process, and the following considerations can contribute to effective media use in the classroom.[6] The first has to do with preparing the learner for the media or materials. Learner readiness for different types of media must be assessed. This is part of the process of identifying characteristics of a group of learners when engaging in curriculum planning and instructional design.

Students can be prepared in several ways for a learning experience utilizing a certain type of media. Discussion to review the extent of students' knowledge of the subject or topic will help them prepare to learn new knowledge, information and concepts. Defining any new terms used in the medium will minimize confusion, and increase understanding. Having previewed the material, the teacher will know just how it should fit into the overall learning structure, and exactly what information students must have prior to using the media in order for them to understand its message fully.

Presenting students with a prepared list of questions ahead of time will alert them to look for specific things in the content of the media or materials. It will help improve their attention focus, and provide more specific parameters within which the new learning will occur.

Carefully planned and designed instructional sequences will have provided students with earlier experiences using various media and materials. These earlier experiences are drawn upon to increase the effectiveness of the current instruction.

Learners should be involved in several ways in the actual presentation of the media or materials. More than just passive viewing of a presentation is required. Learners need to know that they are expected to react to the media, and should have a clear idea of *how* they are expected to react. Internalizing new learning experiences involves effort on the part of the learner. Teacher observation of students' verbal and/or physical response to the information pre-

---

[6]Klasek, *Instructional Media in the Modern School,* p. 40.

sented will indicate the level of their understanding. The extent to which the student applies a new understanding or skill to other learning situations also needs to be assessed.

Media and other learning materials embody a sequentially organized presentation of information within a certain framework. However, it is not always necessary, or even desirable, to start at the beginning and go completely through to the end in exactly the manner prescribed by the medium. Variation in the "beginning-to-end" format can often produce more effective results and help maintain focus on the objective. Ways to do this, for example, include showing only the key parts of the medium instead of the entire package, followed by discussion. Showing a portion of the medium day by day might be, in some instances, more effective than showing it all in one sitting. Or, the medium may be interrupted as it is in progress in order to discuss key points immediately, instead of waiting until the end to discuss them all at once. This allows for closer examination of each part of the whole, and shows how the parts are related to one another.

Another way in which to help students see how the parts relate to the whole is to show them the whole package first, so they can form a general impression. Then show it again, this time in small portions, stopping at critical points to discuss, take notes, and react/respond to what has just been presented.

One technique that will increase students' active participation is to use only the visual portion of the medium, and let them supply their own narration or explanation of what they are seeing. They could then view it again, this time with the audio component, to compare their own work with what the medium actually contained. To increase listening skills, reverse this process, and have students use only the audio portion while they portray what they think is happening. Again, the medium can be used in its entirety when they are done, so the students can visually compare what they did with what actually happened.

A more individualized approach would be to let a student, or small group of students, utilize the media and/or materials, and then prepare a report for the rest of the class.

For additional, creative suggestions on innovative ways to utilize various media in the instructional process, it is suggested that the reader consult the following source:

Glogau, L.; Krause, E.; and Wexler, M., *Developing a Successful Elementary School Media Center*. West Nyack, N.Y.: Parker Publishing Company, Inc., 1972. Chapter 8: "The Appropriate Use and Misuse of Audio-Visual Equipment," pp. 203–209.

Learning experiences involving the use of media can be extended and reinforced with additional follow-up activities. Group discussion is one way, individual written response or reaction to the learning experience is another. The intent is to draw out the experiences the learner has had, and determine what they mean to him.

Student demonstrations of the application of a technique, task, skill, concept or idea can reinforce the learning. Active student participation of this nature requires the student to think through carefully what he or she is presenting so that it can be clearly understood by others.

An individual, small group, or class project can be a logical outgrowth of a mediated learning experience. This could range anywhere from the construction of a model to a service project, depending on the objective. A clay model will help represent a learner's understanding of the geography of mountains. A school store in which the students develop, market, and sell a product will help give meaning to basic business concepts, and provides hands-on "manufacturing" experience. Project outcomes may be tangible or intangible; or usually a combination of both.

Additional instructional media can be used to expand and reinforce the information presented by the original choice of media. These can include assigned outside reading; the written word is one form of instructional media. However, care must be taken to be sure that all the pieces of the media puzzle fit together in a logical way.

One other way to increase the depth and breadth of the instruction presented to the learners is through the use of outside resources. These can include community resources, business and industry, specialists or consultants, field trips, and people with special talents or experiences. In planning any activities that serve to extend and enrich the mediated learning taking place in the classroom, the teacher and librarian are limited only by the extent of their resourcefulness, imagination, and creativity. Also, the students may have some very good suggestions of their own. The more students are included in determining the direction of their own learning, the more actively involved in it they will become. This will contribute to increased initiative in future and continued learning endeavors.

One instructional strategy that has been receiving increased attention recently, particularly in regard to the appropriate use of media and materials in instruction, is the inquiry method. "Learning by inquiry is a basic part of an instructional program designed to enable students to learn how to think rather than be telling them what to think."[7] Through use of the inquiry method in teaching, students learn how to ask questions and analyze information. This process involves skill in defining, observing, classifying, generalizing, verifying, drawing conclusions, making judgments and communicating findings. Students learn how to find creative ways to solve problems. This method works best when students have the opportunity to participate in and respond to many different kinds of learning experiences. An instructional strategy based on the inquiry method provides the perfect setting for a broad range of learning experiences involving a wide variety of media.

Shepherd and Ragan point out three phases of inquiry: exploration, invention, and expansion, and the supportive role instructional media may play in one or more of these phases.[8] In order for media to support the **exploration** phase of inquiry, they must:

1. Be within the previous experience of the learner.
2. Involve the learner in activities such as observing, classifying, manipulating, comparing and contrasting.
3. Have flexibility, so that it may be used in more than one way. For instance, some learners may classify by color, some by shape, etc.
4. Not have any explanation of the information presented. In this way, no restrictions are placed on explorations on the part of the learner.
5. Be appropriate to the developmental level of the learner (moving from concrete to abstract.)

---

[7]Ruth Ann Davies, *The School Library Media Program: Instructional Force for Learning,* 3rd ed. (New York and London: R.R. Bowker Company, 1979), p. 54.
[8]Gene D. Shepherd and William B. Ragan, *Modern Elementary Curriculum,* 6th ed. (Holt, Rinehart and Winston, 1982), pp. 134–135.

In order for media to support the **invention** phase of inquiry they must:

1. Be divergent in the explanation of the information it depicts. It should encourage the learner to think, and look for more than one explanation or reason, and for interrelationships before drawing his own conclusions.
2. Have an unexpected element of information that may appear to conflict with the initial conclusions of the learner. This is to encourage further thinking and exploration before drawing final conclusions.
3. It should involve the learner in either a physical or intellectual manner, or a combination of both whenever possible.

In order for media to support the **expansion** phase of inquiry they must:

1. Suggest ways of testing the hypothesis or conclusions it may present.
2. Provide or suggest ways to collect and organize information resulting from exploration on the part of the learner, and provide suggestions on how it can be interpreted.
3. Provide suggestions for application of skills, concepts, or information learned to other situations, both similar to and different from the one presented by the media.
4. Provide enough information to allow the learner to verify or modify his conclusions (hypotheses).

Not all media will be able to fully meet this exhaustive set of criteria, but this does not mean that the criteria should be disregarded. As mentioned earlier, it may sometimes be more beneficial to utilize a portion of the media package rather than the entire package. The same principle applies here. This stringent set of requirements can be a valuable aid to the teacher and librarian in evaluating the choice and use of media in instruction.

The underlying purpose of well planned instruction incorporating the use of many types of media is to teach students *how to learn*. They are encouraged to acquire not only information, but, more importantly, to develop skills and insights as well. They should be led to the discovery of ideas, and learn to formulate general principles and concepts. The extent of a student's knowledge is not as important as knowing *how* to "find out more," and expand his or her knowledge base.

Teachers are no longer content or comfortable with merely imparting knowledge. This represents a somewhat shallow, one-dimensional learning environment for the students, and does not truly equip them with skills they can actively apply in their own lives. Instead of confining the student within a limited set of parameters, the inquiry method supported by a strong media base can provide learning experiences of unlimited variety.

Pupil Experience Levels and Media Use

Children's experiences in the instructional setting should involve listening, observing and doing. The best learning results from a balanced combination of all three elements. Having learners sit and listen all day long is an easy trap to fall into, but this passive approach leaves much to be desired. Young children with limited perceptions need learning experiences that are structured to begin at a concrete level and move towards the abstract. The use of various types of media can support the development of the child's experiential base. Learning experiences can become increasingly sophisticated as the learner's concept level expands. The child can move from seeing and doing to increased levels of abstract thinking and understanding. Dale developed a useful guide that can be applied to the selection of appropriate media based on the learner's present level of experiences and the purpose of instruction. The different levels of the guide move from the most concrete to the most abstract.[9]

Doing
  a. Direct, purposeful experience—interaction with objects, materials, people, etc.
  b. Contrived experiences—models, mock-ups, simulations.

---

[9]Edgar Dale, *Audiovisual Methods in Teaching,* revised ed. (New York: The Dryden Press, 1954), pp. 42–56.

    c. Dramatized experiences—role playing, puppets, plays, a reconstruction of real experience.

Doing and Observing

    d. Demonstrations—may involve doing as well as observing.

    e. Field trips—doing and observing.

    f. Exhibits—"ready-made" or "home-made."

Moving Toward Most Abstract

    g. Television, motion pictures—learner is somewhat removed from actual experiences depicted on film.

    h. Recordings, radio, still pictures—involving increased abstractness, use of only one sense (sight or sound).

    i. Visual symbols—chalkboards, maps, charts, diagrams.

    j. Verbal symbols—most abstract, though they are used in conjunction with each of the other items.

A suggestion for using these guidelines as an aid to media and materials selection is to go toward the low (doing) end as far as necessary to ensure learning, but go toward the high (most abstract) end as far as possible for the most efficient learning. The different items in this guide are not really separate from one another. They only represent increasing levels of abstractness and are meant to be integrated as much as possible. Students will constantly be moving up and down between the levels or through combinations of levels as they learn new things, and then go on to apply their learning to new situations. In other words, students do not begin their education functioning only at the lower end of the scale and complete it at the high end of the scale. Each new learning experience at any age will require movement among the different levels.

Summary

Information, ideas, and concepts are effectively presented to learners by the appropriate combination of people, media and materials, and teaching methodologies. It is important to utilize instructional media in an appropriate manner: media can never substitute for the human element in a teaching/learning situation, nor are they used simply for entertainment. This is not to say that learning can't or shouldn't be fun. The appropriate use of media can and should help to provide a learning experience that is worthwhile as well as enjoyable.

The right use of the proper materials and resources can enhance and contribute a special dimension to the learning experience. Instructional media can greatly increase learning efficiency and interest levels. Learners who have the opportunity to interact with a wide variety of media at different experiential levels are also afforded a larger scope of creative responses than those who have had only "chalk and talk." Systematic use of media in the instructional process provides for concrete experiences first moving toward increasingly abstract learning sequences.

The use of instructional media is not an end in itself. It is the student's reaction and response to the media that makes the difference. If instructional media have played a role, even a small one, in helping a student learn how to learn, or teaching him to think for himself, then they have served its purpose.

The teacher who is responsive to the role he or she plays in helping shape the future of students will make every effort to fulfill this obligation. The informed, responsible, and appropriate use of a wide variety of media and materials in the educational process is one way of accomplishing this.

References

Bender, David R. "Networking and School Library Media Programs," *School Library Journal* 26 (November 1979): 29–32.

Chisholm, Margaret E., and Ely, Donald P. *Media Personnel in Education: A Competency Approach.* Englewood Cliffs, N.J.: Prentice-Hall, Inc., 1976.

Clarke, Norman F. "Library Education in an Era of Media," *Contemporary Education* 41 (November 1969): 61–66.

Dale, Edgar. *Audiovisual Methods in Teaching.* Revised ed. New York: The Dryden Press, 1954.

Ellington, Henry. *Producing Teaching Materials: A Handbook for Teachers and Trainers.* London: Kegan Page Ltd., and New York: Nichols Publishing Company, 1985.

Glogau, L.; Krause, E.; and Wexler, M. *Developing a Successful Elementary School Media Center.* West Nyack, N.Y.: Parker Publishing Company, Inc., 1972.

Klasek, Charles B. *Instructional Media in the Modern School.* Lincoln, Neb.: Professional Educators Publications, Inc., 1972.

Shepherd, Gene D., and Ragan, William B. *Modern Elementary Curriculum.* 6th ed. New York: Holt, Rinehart and Winston, 1982.

Talmage, Harriet. "The Textbook as Arbiter of Curriculum and Instruction," *The Elementary School Journal* 73 (October 1972): 20–25.

Wittich, Walter A., and Schuller, Charles F. *Instructional Technology: Its Nature and Use.* 6th ed. New York: Harper and Row, 1979.

Chapter 8

LOCATING AND USING MEDIA

THIS CHAPTER PROVIDES a review of the essential skills needed to be able to use the school library media center effectively and efficiently. Different ways in which media can be a part of the instructional setting are addressed, and the underlying theoretical base for use of media is also discussed.

The school library media center has a wealth of media, materials, resources and services available for the teacher to use in order to provide the best learning experiences possible for the students. These are presented in the list below to help provide a comprehensive view of the scope of the library media center. Not all types of materials will be found in all centers, but these items are representative of the materials, resources and services that can be found in the majority of centers. Specific items not readily available can usually be requested through interlibrary loan.

Materials and Resources

- books (all types)
- periodicals (newspapers, magazines)
- filmstrips/filmstrip projector/filmstrip viewer
- 16mm films/16mm film projector
- slides/slide projector
- video tapes/video tape player/video cameras
- computers/software
- television
- slide-tape kits
- book-record kits
- filmstrip-cassette, or filmstrip-record kits

— audio tapes/tape recorder
— disc recordings/record player
— study prints
— slides
— realia
— 8mm film loops/film loop projector
— maps (flat and relief)
— globes
— microfiche cards/microfiche reader
— microfilm/microfilm reader
— transparencies/overhead projector
— pictures/opaque projector
— radio programs
— posters
— charts
— flannel board and materials
— vertical file (pamphlets, clippings)
— laminator
— copy machine (ditto, Xerox, mimeo)
— Thermofax (transparencies, spirit masters)
— dry mount press
— tacking iron
— paper cutter
— slide camera
— tape splicer
— primary typewriter
— letter kits

Teachers also need to have skills in operating equipment: movie projectors, video tape players, video cameras, computers, etc.

The classroom teacher should be familiar not only with the in-school resources available through the media center, but should also have an awareness of out-of-school resources (community, etc.) and the human resources (people with expertise in certain special areas) that are readily available to them. They should know how to access out-of-school resources. This may require a certain amount of aggressiveness and creativity to get what is needed.

Teachers have a professional obligation to keep up on current trends and practices in the field. To this end, they need to be familiar with the professional collection available to them, and make regular use of it. This includes such materials as these:

— professional books and periodicals
— curriculum guides, courses of study
— community resource guides (or develop their own, to share with other teachers and/or place in the media center)
— grade level textbooks, teachers' manuals for basic and supplementary use
— non-print materials (films, audio tapes, video tapes available through professional organizations)
— pamphlets
— keep current on information on workshops, continuing education, college courses, special institutes
— professional organizations, newsletters, announcements, miscellaneous releases
— government documents
— *Education Index, Current Index to Journals in Education (CIJE), Educational Resources Information Center (ERIC),* etc.

Chances are that not every item on this list will be available to the teacher through the school library media center. However, teachers should at least know how to gain access to these materials for their own continued professional growth.

The many services available through the media center often go unused because teachers are not aware of them. Here are some examples of such services:

1) media production services

2) instructional services:
   — supplemental materials sent to the classroom
   — introduction of materials (by the librarian) centered around classroom units of work
   — assistance on student research projects (individual and group)
   — teaching and/or reinforcement of library media skills related to classroom units of work

  — book talks related to units of work
  — bibliographies compiled on selected topics of interest
  — information on new materials added to the collection
3) consultation services:
  — curriculum development
  — recommendations on ways of using specific materials
  and equipment
  — assistance in selection of appropriate media for instruction

   It is essential that the classroom teacher have a working knowledge and thorough understanding of the organizational patterns and schemes of the school library media center. It is also essential that the teacher possess information access skills, and be competent in applying them in terms of the teacher's responsibility to the students. This responsibility means providing the highest possible quality teaching and learning experiences for the students. It also means having the ability to teach these skills to students in order to help them in their learning, both in school and out.
   Teachers should be familiar with the arrangement of the materials found in a media center. This includes the following:

A. Books, location of:
  1) easy and picture books
  2) non-fiction (organized by subject and arranged in numerical order)
  3) fiction (arranged in alphabetical order according to author)
  4) biography (arranged in alphabetical order according to biographee)
  5) ten main divisions of the Dewey Decimal Classification System:
  000   General Works
  100   Philosophy
  200   Religion
  300   Social Sciences
  400   Languages
  500   Pure Sciences
  600   Technology
  700   The Arts

800   Literature
900   History

B. Location and arrangement of:
— filmstrips
— recordings
— picture file
— periodicals
— vertical file
— transparency file

C. Reference materials:
1) dictionaries;
   — use of guide words
   — tabs
   — abridged and unabridged
   — appendices of
   — antonyms, homonyms, synonyms, syllabication
   — types of special dictionaries available; geographical, biographical, picture dictionary, etc.
2) encyclopedias;
   — location in library media center
   — types of information found in
   — use of index
   — use of cross reference and related subject references
   — yearbooks
3) indices—examples include:
   — *Index to Children's Poetry,* Brewton
   — *Index to Fairy Tales, Myths and Legends,* Eastman
   — *Subject Index to Books for Primary Grades* and *Subject Index to Books for Intermediate Grades,* Eakin
   — *Index to Young Reader's Collective Biographies,* Silverman
   — *Junior Books of Authors, More Junior Authors*
   — *Children's Literature Review*
   — *Abridged Readers' Guide to Periodical Literature*
4) location of periodicals, magazines, newspapers
5) location of atlases, almanacs
6) use of non-print media for references, such as filmstrips, records, cassettes, film loops, maps, globes, study prints

D. Other types of non-print materials:
   —films
   —television
   —video tapes
   —art prints
   —microfiche/microfilm
   —slides
   —realia

E. Card catalog, location of:
   — types of cards: author card, title card, subject card
   — use of cross-reference cards (*See, See also*)
   — cards for non-print materials
   — interpret the following information on a catalog card: author, title, call number, publisher, copyright date, medium, number of pages (if applicable), whether or not there are illustrations (if applicable)

F. Additional skills teachers should possess, at least to some extent, include the following:
   1) knowledge of how to access the ERIC (*Educational Resources Information Center*) system
   2) skill in using CIJE (*Current Index to Journals in Education*)
   3) an understanding of the Library of Congress cataloging system
   4) familiarity with the print and non-print curriculum materials available for specific grades in various subject areas
   5) use of interlibrary loan service
   6) awareness and use of additional information sources outside of the school library media center
   7) keep informed about and make recommendations for new acquisitions for the center

Basis for Media Use

It is important for teachers to develop a conceptual base for the use of media in the instructional process. Media should be regarded as tools that are as basic as books in the instructional process. Media are partners with, not replacements for, the traditional classroom textbook. They are also intended to be used as *equal* partners with books, not supplements.

There are several underlying purposes for the use of media as equals in the instructional process. Use of media can stimulate student interest in a manner that a textbook may not always be able to, resulting in a heightened perception of concepts, ideas, and the world at large. Use of media can assist in the active building and broadening of concepts. It can also help to improve the learning process, because it adds variety, and can provide a much wider range of experiences than reliance on the textbook alone.

There are some general principles that can be helpful in guiding the use of media in the instructional process. The selection of media should always be based on valid objectives, and should also take into account the characteristics of the learners with whom it will be used.

The development of learner readiness prior to the use of a particular media format must be considered. Students may not always have the prior experience necessary to get the most out of the media being considered for use. Attention to this point, and adequate preparation of the learners will enable students to participate more effectively in the learning experience.

Sometimes, the physical requirements for use of the media are not examined until the teacher is ready to actually use them. It is especially important that details concerning the physical facilities and conditions for using the desired media format be worked out ahead of time. There are two reasons for doing this. One is to help safeguard the materials and equipment. The other is to provide for economy of time, and most important of all, optimum learner attention. Having the physical set-up prepared ahead of time eliminates potential distractions, and allows learning to continue uninterrupted.

When learners use media in the instructional process, they may need to receive some direction in reacting to the media. The teacher must be cognizant of the need to provide guidance for the *action* taken by the learner as a result of experiencing the media.

A final principle, equally important with all the others, is to subject both the media and the way in which they are used to continual evaluation. This can be in terms of the appropriateness of the media for a certain group of students, the technique the teacher employed in using the media, and the overall level of effectiveness, as measured by the attainment of the stated objective(s).

Creating and Modifying Media and Materials

The creation of media and materials to meet the needs of learning situations for which there are no suitable materials readily available requires the teacher to have certain technical skills in addition to a thorough knowledge of all components of the instructional program. *Appropriate* media and materials can be created only with a clear picture of the entire learning program. The technical skills referred to involve not only the capability of creating the tools necessary to put the instructional plans into motion, but the ability to match the media with the objectives. Media competence involves more than just equipment operations skills. It has more to do with successfully blending theory and practice, and coming up with workable, effective combinations.

There are some general principles and suggestions that are helpful in the creation of media and materials to meet a specific need. The first, as stated earlier, and probably the most important, is to have a clear understanding of the instructional objectives, and to be certain that the objectives are valid. The media and materials are created to help meet the objective. The objective is never determined by what media or materials happen to be available. A comparison of media and materials currently available with the objectives of the curriculum will help pinpoint weak areas in the media collection, and allow for the development of a long-range plan for creating needed materials, or planning for appropriate acquisitions.

Before preparing to develop materials, the teacher should gather anything that can be found that is related to the topic and/or the instructional medium. Both print and non-print materials can be useful in the creation of something new to meet an instructional need. Information or ideas for ways to present it can always be gleaned from old materials that can no longer be used because they are outdated or in poor condition. Creating, like learning, does not occur in a vacuum. The more raw materials a teacher can collect and draw from, the more comprehensive and complete his or her own materials will be. This does not mean that it is necessary to include every last scrap of raw material in the creation of new materials. Presentation of information should be comprehensive without being cluttered by unnecessary details. An examination of the way in which commercial materials have been prepared can also provide the teacher with ideas on how to design media or materials.

The creation of media and materials may not always happen in a sudden burst. As the teacher gathers and examines raw materials from which to create his or her own, some "thinking time" should be allowed to let ideas germinate and begin to develop. Long-range planning will build in time for just such a process. Also, as the teacher creates media or materials, a determination needs to be made of what *type* of materials are best suited to the students.

Before the teacher actually creates the media or materials, certain questions should be answered:

What elements need to be included?

How many students will be using the materials?

What type of learning materials will be most effective?

How can needed information/instruction be provided?

How will students' work be evaluated?[1]

Careful attention to the answers to each question listed above will provide the teacher with a clear set of parameters within which to work.

> Consideration must be given to the various parts that need to be included in most learning materials such as a title, stated purpose(s) or objective(s), directions, and evaluation for learning.
>
> After completing any learning materials, they need to be checked to make sure that
>
> — language is simple and understandable;
> — materials are in fact meeting the stated objective(s) or purpose(s);
> — activities are appropriate for the age, needs, and/or interests of the students.

---

[1]Alice R. Seaver, *Library Media Skills: Strategies for Instructing Primary Students* (Littleton, Colo.: Libraries Unlimited, Inc., 1984), p. 80.

Directions need to be simple and clear, and the understanding
and reading levels of the students who will be using the [media/
materials] need to be considered.[2]

Attention to the factors listed above will help ensure a layout
that the students can understand, use, and follow with ease. Once
they are ready, media/materials should be field-tested with a small
group of students to work out any bugs that may show up during
use. This will help eliminate unnecessary or unworkable parts or
sections, and also point up where something should be added or
changed. After the media or materials have been revised based on
the results of the pilot test, they should be subjected to another
evaluation, in their new form. Evaluation and revision are ongoing
processes, not only to keep the media or materials up-to-date, but
to determine their appropriateness for each new group of students
who will be using them. To this effect, they should be sturdily
constructed to last for an extended period of time.

Broad Categories of Learning Media and Materials

This section is a general discussion of nine different categories of
learning media other than the textbook. It is intended only to provide basic information, since each of these categories is treated
more extensively in other sources. Each has its proper place in the
instructional process, and each requires certain skills of the teacher
in order to be put to effective use. As noted in the previous section,
a combination of skills is needed in order to integrate these various
media successfully into instruction. The teacher must have skills in
planning and organizing for the instructional program as well as in
materials and media production. This requires a degree of resourcefulness, and is an area in which creativity knows no limits.
    The brief discussion of each category should help the teacher
begin to consider the various ways in which each medium, or
combination of media, might be put to use in the instructional
process. The nine different categories are: printed and/or dupli-
cated materials; non-projected display materials, pictures and
graphics; still projections; audio materials; audio/visual materials;

---

[2]Ibid.

television and motion pictures; multi-dimensional materials; community resources; and computers.

Printed and/or Duplicated Materials

This type of material, often called a handout, can include such things as a work sheet, notes on a lesson, or a graphic to support the learning. Materials of this type should always be used to help reach specific objectives, never as busy work. Handouts distributed to an entire group of learners can help improve the effectiveness as well as the efficiency of the instructional process. If the handout is a work sheet of some sort, it allows the learner a degree of participation in what might otherwise be a passive learning experience (the lecture method, for example.)

Besides playing an instructional support role, this type of material can also be the center of a specific learning experience and the means by which the information is conveyed. Printed materials can provide direction and guidance on how to do a particular exercise, or additional explanatory material. This type of material can also be used, and often is, to support other types of learning materials and media.

When designing printed material, the teacher must know the instructional role the material is intended to play (for example, a support role, or as a central point of the instruction), have a good basic plan for the material, and pay careful attention to its writing and physical design. This last consideration can be *the* determining factor in the successful use of the material.

Non-Projected Displays, Pictures, and Graphics

When used in class instruction, this medium most often plays a support role in the instructional process. In an individualized learning setting, however, non-projected materials can play a key role, to the point of actually providing the object of study.

Pictures and graphics can be useful in conveying concepts and information. Regular use of these materials in the instructional process helps in the development of a student's visual literacy. Students have the opportunity to develop their ability to interpret visual messages and information, and also their sequencing skills. Student response, both verbally and in writing, to visuals will allow the teacher to evaluate the student development in these areas. However, visual clutter should be guarded against; it is often better to have a few well chosen pictures or graphics than too many. Pictures and graphics convey information in a one-dimensional fashion. Other non-projected learning materials include multi-dimensional displays. They can be used to motivate, promote concept development, or summarize information that has been presented. A variety of materials can be used: a combination of pictures, graphics, and three-dimensional objects to convey information and provide explanations.

In creating learning displays, the following points should be kept in mind:

1. Study displays are learning experiences.
2. A good display results from good planning.
3. Study displays should be related to the subject being studied and the interests of the learners. The best study displays involve learners and entice them to search further for information on a subject.
4. The best learning displays command attention; communicate concepts, facts, and insights; and develop enthusiasm for the subject being studied.
5. A good learning display has a good physical organization and layout.

Study displays should be a joint effort by teachers and pupils. Often pupils learn more from making displays than from looking at them.

Study displays should be evaluated according to three criteria: whether they achieve their purpose, the effectiveness of their design, and the degree to which they involve students.[3]

Still Projections

Still projections include such things as slides, opaque projections, filmstrips, and transparencies. These are the items most often found in the classroom setting. Microfilm and microfiche are also examples of still-projected material, although they are not widely used in a classroom setting. (These materials are better suited to individualized instruction.) Still projections play a useful support

[3]Walter A. Wittich and Charles F. Schuller, *Instructional Technology: Its Nature and Use*, 6th ed. (New York: Harper and Row, 1979), p. 136.

role in both large- and small-group instruction. In individualized instruction, they can be especially useful when used together with audio materials.

Still-projected materials can be an effective means of conveying information, concepts, and ideas to the learner. However, their effectiveness is determined by two things. One is objectives that are clearly defined and understood by both teacher and student. The technical quality of the material also has a direct bearing on how effectively it is able to communicate the information it contains. Effectiveness is further determined by *how* the material is used. Preparing and motivating the class, attention to good projection conditions, and appropriate follow-up activities are all important.

Additional advantages of using still projections are that they can be studied for whatever length of time is necessary to derive and understand the information conveyed; they are usually readily available in most school media centers, and generally are not prohibitively costly. The equipment necessary for projection is simple to operate. In addition to the wide variety of still-projected materials available commercially, teachers can design their own. The design and use of still-projected material, while requiring careful planning and layout, does not involve the levels of complexity encountered in the design and use of certain other types of instructional media.

Audio Materials

Audio materials come in the form of tape recordings, records, and radio. Though often used in combination with visual materials, they can also serve a valuable purpose as a "stand alone" medium. The strengths and advantages of using audio materials alone are often overlooked.

In large-group instruction, audio materials can function in a support role, can be the actual means of instruction, or can serve as the promoter of further activity by the learner. Students may react or respond to what they have heard in a variety of ways; discussion, role playing, or further research, for example. In small-group instruction, audio materials can serve as the main means by which to convey information to the students. They can also be used as a guide for learners, to help them through an exercise, or provide the means by which the students interact with one another to further their learning.

In individualized instruction, audio materials serve these same purposes. They can also provide the means by which the student interacts with the material itself. An example of this is a foreign language lab. In individualized instruction, as in small and large groups, audio materials may be used alone or in an audio/visual combination.

Use of audio materials alone call for the learner to do several things. The learner must not only be able to hear the material, but must also know how to *listen* to it. After listening to it, a response of some kind is necessary so that mastery of the content of the audio material can be evaluated.

Students are surrounded by an overabundance of visual stimuli in their everyday lives. This heavy reliance on the visual often down plays the importance of learning how to listen to gain new information, ideas, or concepts. Many listen to the radio for enjoyment, but in a passive way. No response is required of the listener. Listening to gain information requires a response from the listener, in reaction to the message or information. Special attention must be paid to the development and improvement of listening skills. Audio materials alone serve this purpose very well, but the teacher and students must both know what type of response is expected after using this medium.

Student interest in audio materials can be motivated by letting students create their own. Equipment is readily available and easily operated. Providing students with structured opportunities to create their own audio materials can be an effective teaching strategy.

When teachers are selecting audio materials to use in the instructional process, they should look for materials that have clear explanations and directions. Information presented should be straightforward and accurate. If a task is required of the learner, it should be clearly indicated in the audio material, and there must be means by which both teachers and students can evaluate their progress. Also, students should be encouraged to apply the skills or information creatively to new situations.

Audio/Visual Materials

Audio/visual materials can be used effectively in all types of instruction; large-group, small-group, and individualized. The computer has recently replaced audio/visual material as being the most effective tool for individualized instruction, but this has not lessened the value of audio/visual materials. They are still valid, widely used, and far from obsolete.

Audio/visual materials may take the form of slide/tape, slide/record, tape/picture, tape/filmstrip, etc. There are many possible combinations of audio and visual materials, but the combinations need to work well together in order to be able to convey information effectively. Teachers should bear this in mind when reviewing audio/visual materials or planning production of their own materials.

As with all media, planning for the use of audio/visual materials begins with a clear set of objectives and a careful study of the characteristics of the learners. Some combinations may work better than others for specific applications, and teachers need to know this before selecting available material or designing and producing their own. The content of the materials may be a factor in determining what combinations work best. Teachers designing their own materials need to have a detailed knowledge of the topic being presented so that they can prepare a well written "script" for the presentation. Timing, and the coordination of the spoken word with the visual presentation, must be worked out. Materials should then be field-tested, and modified as necessary.

Television and Films

Television and films lend themselves well to large-group classroom instruction. The use of 16mm films for individualized instruction, though more difficult, can be accomplished with the proper facilities, specifically a separate viewing room. 8mm film loops may be better suited to this instructional mode.

> In any teaching situation, it is the teachers' responsibility to create opportunities for learners to become *involved* in the learning experience and *respond* to it by using newfound information in constructive, creative ways. This is particularly true in regard to televised learning experiences.[4]

Television viewing is usually a passive experience. It is more difficult with this particular medium than with others to draw students actively into the learning experience. Therefore, use of this

---

[4]Wittich and Schuller, *Instructional Technology: Its Nature and Use*, p. 260.

medium requires that the teacher construct and provide the interaction necessary to make the learning meaningful. This is easier to accomplish with 16mm films. Students need to be prepared for a film the same way they need to be prepared for a televised learning experience. However, 16mm films create a somewhat different "atmosphere" and subsequent response from students than television viewing.

Prior to viewing a film or television, students need to know what the content will be, and how it relates to what they are already studying. They also need to know what is expected of them after they view the film or television program.

Consideration must be given to the physical facilities in which the film or television presentation is being viewed. Students must be able to see and hear the presentation clearly. And they (as well as their teachers) need to understand that this is a learning experience, not simply entertainment. This is not to say that it can't be enjoyable, simply that appropriate use of films and television ensures that they are a carefully integrated part of the total instructional experience, not an incidental.

Multi-Dimensional Materials

Multi-dimensional teaching materials include models, specimens, mock-ups and dioramas; concrete objects that can be seen and handled by the student. They are often a good substitute for first-hand experience, especially when it may be impractical in terms of time or distance for students to participate in a direct learning experience. The design and construction of multi-dimensional learning materials can provide valuable learning experiences for the students. They must have a full grasp of the concept, idea, or information to be presented in a display in order to be able to plan and construct it. Students can also learn more from objects they can manipulate, take apart and put together, and see from various angles.

When creating and using multi-dimensional materials, attention should be given to a balance among the types of materials used to construct a display. The design and color of materials used in the display must be carefully planned. They should help communicate the information in the display, not obstruct it. More sophisticated displays may involve the use of light and motion. Again, these should be an integral part of the display, not just a flashy element that really serves no purpose. A provision should be made for interacting with the display where feasible, to promote learning by doing.

Community Resources

The community can provide a valuable, interesting, and often unusual learning medium. Two-way interaction is possible: the classroom can extend into the community, or the community into the classroom. It allows students to have first-hand experiences with the real world. No other instructional medium can provide this total realism. All other media formats generally provide substitute experiences that are as close an approximation of reality as possible. Community study is a direct link to the real world.

Use of community resources requires careful planning, and students should be involved in the planning process as much as possible. The use of community resources, as with all other media, should be an integral part of the total instructional program. It is extremely important that students know not only what they are expected to learn, but also how they are expected to act and interact with this unique resource. The students represent themselves as well as their school, and can play an important role in promoting good school-community relations.

Resources and opportunities for learning found within the community are many. Field trips can be made to local museums, factories, etc. People in the community may have special talents or experiences they can share with students, or they can help form a panel to discuss specific topics.

Community materials include newspapers, Chamber of Commerce publications, and libraries. Those who provide services for the community can be interviewed: policemen, postal workers, local government officials, those who work to keep the community clean, etc. Various service clubs and organizations can be found in any community, and can provide valuable information and insights into the workings of the community. Students can conduct their own service projects, or do a field study on such things as pollution or local housing problems. Current events within the local community can provide interesting sources of study.

Teachers have a responsibility to know the community in which

they work. Well planned experiences involving community resources can provide students with some of their most valuable and
meaningful learning.

Computers

The computer is among the latest, and most highly visible, media innovations to arrive on the educational scene. It is a unique
learning tool and has become a familiar fixture in the home and the
workplace as well as the school. It has altered the definition of
literacy, which once included only reading and writing. Computers
have come to play such an important role in our society that those
who are unfamiliar with their capabilities and use are at a great
disadvantage. Children are growing up with them; it is the adults
who have the catching up to do.

Computers are not intended to take the place of anything, least
of all the teacher. They *are* intended to contribute to the instructional process, and can do this in a way that no other medium can.

Computers can serve several instructional functions. One is for
drill and practice: an electronic work sheet. The computer can also
play the role of the teacher. Students can learn new material as
presented by the computer (best for individualized instruction) instead of the teacher. Computers can increase student motivation
and participation in the learning process through the use of games
and simulations. A game lets the student interact with the computer, an element of competition is introduced, and the student's success in the competition is determined by the level of learning demonstrated as the game is played. A simulation can provide students
with a representation of real experiences that are not feasible in the
classroom setting. Active participation is required and the student
learns about something by, in a sense, doing it. Computers are also
a useful tool in the storage and retrieval of information. They are not
replacing other, more traditional methods of storing information
(i.e., a library); they are simply making them more difficult.

Computers have been accused of dehumanizing the classroom.
If they were to become the sole means of instruction, this would be
true. What they really represent is one more way in which to make
learning more interesting and efficient. Computers are not intended
to be used to the exclusion of all else in the classroom; they should
be used in conjunction with other media formats and teaching strat-

egies, and give the teacher one more option to choose from in constructing learning experiences best suited to the needs of the student.

Summary

An understanding of the basic organizational schemes of the library will allow both teachers and students to operate in them more effectively. Teachers need to possess and use information access skills. These can be applied for purposes of professional growth, and for research and reference work in preparation for a new unit of classroom study. Continual application of these skills in the teaching process will help maintain high-quality classroom instruction, and represents a commitment to excellence in teaching. Teachers must also be able to teach these skills to their students. This is a significant function of the process of learning how to learn.

In order for teachers to achieve this goal, they must be familiar with a wide range of instructional media, and understand their application in the teaching process.

> You must use each medium for its unique features. There is no substitute for a book when *only* the printed word can create a certain world; there is no substitute for the film when *only* the motion picture can create a certain world; there is no substitute for the recording when *only* the spoken work or musical form can create a certain world, etc. to the obviously reassuring fact that there is no substitute for the human being when his presence alone can create a certain world.[5]

Above all, we must never lose sight of the fact that education is an enterprise whose central element is people. It is those who are served—the students, and those who serve them—the teachers. The teacher has been, and will continue to be, the most important and necessary instructional medium there is.

---

[5]D. Marie Grieco, "Communications . . . The Undiscovered Country," *Instructional Materials Centers,* eds. Neville P. Pearson and Lucius Butler (Burgess Publishing Company, 1969), p. 75.

References

Cuban, Larry. *Teachers and Machines: The Classroom Use of Technology Since 1920.* New York and London: Teachers College Press, 1986.

Davies, Ruth Ann. *The School Library Media Program: Instructional Force for Excellence,* 3rd ed. New York and London: R.R. Bowker Company, 1979.

Ellington, Henry. *Producing Teaching Materials: A Handbook for Teachers and Trainers.* London: Kegan Page Ltd., and New York: Nichols Publishing Company, 1985.

Erikson, Carlton W.H. *Administering Instructional Media Programs.* New York: The Macmillan Co., 1968.

Seaver, Alice A. *Library Media Skills: Strategies for Instructing Primary Students.* Little, Colo.: Libraries Unlimited, Inc., 1984.

Wittich, Walter A., and Schuller, Charles F. *Instructional Technology: Its Nature and Use,* 6th ed. New York: Harper and Row, 1979.

INDEX